A NEW ERA IN BANKING

A NEW ERA IN BANKING

BANKING

The Landscape After the Battle

Angel Berges,
Mauro F. Guillén,
Juan Pedro Moreno
and
Emilio Ontiveros

bibliomotion
books + media

First published by Bibliomotion, Inc.
39 Harvard Street
Brookline, MA 02445
Tel: 617-934-2427
www.bibliomotion.com

Printed in the United States of America

10   9   8   7   6   5

First Paperback Edition

ISBN 978-1-62956-161-5

The Library of Congress has cataloged the hardcover edition as follows:

Library of Congress Cataloging-in-Publication Data

Bergés Lobera, Angel, 1955–
   A new era in banking : the landscape after the battle / Angel Berges, Mauro F. Guillén, Juan Pedro Moreno, Emilio Ontiveros.
      pages cm
   Summary: "A New Era in Banking: The Landscape After the Battle identifies the main drivers of change at the heart of this wholesale transformation of the financial services industry. It examines the complex challenge for financial institutions to de-risk business models, reconnect with customers, and approach stakeholder value creation"—Provided by publisher.
      ISBN 978-1-62956-040-3 (hardback) — ISBN 978-1-62956-041-0 (ebook) — ISBN 978-1-62956-042-7 (enhanced ebook)
   1. Financial services industry.   2. Banks and banking.   3. Finance.   4. Financial institutions.   I. Title.
   HG173.B467 2014
   332.1—dc23
                              2014022541

Contents

Foreword

Richard Lumb, Group Chief Executive of Accenture's Financial Services operating group

The agenda of the financial services industry has been dominated by the financial crisis and its ramifications for the past six years. The collapse of Lehman Brothers was a watershed event for the financial system and for banking in particular. However, it would be a mistake to think that the reaction to the financial crisis, in itself, is the main determinant for the future of banking. The forces that are shaping the banking landscape range across the economic, political, demographic, and technological arenas.

We are moving into a very different world, which banks need to prepare for. Banks face a full agenda of challenges and new opportunities that impact who their customers will be, what they want, and how banks will compete to serve them. And these changes are both profound and dynamic. The banking industry faces a period of unprecedented change and an opportunity to re-architect banking businesses to be ready for the future. This is why Accenture has collaborated on the development of this book, an examination of the changes impacting banks and how to address these changes.

The financial crisis was the largest and most severe crisis to hit financial services in the era of global market integration, but it was not homogeneous in its impact. And while many of the contributing causes were global, such as imbalances in global financial flows and the trends toward market liberalization, the impacts were centered on Western banks and financial markets. Many emerging markets' banking systems, as well as those in select developed countries, flourished and expanded during this period. And many of the new giants of banking come from these countries. While the response to reregulation has seen unprecedented global agreement on the principles for global reform, the rules and implementation are diverse and national in character.

In addition to rebuilding banking after the crisis, the world must adapt to a range of extraordinary changes. Banks must restructure, not to go back to basics but to move forward into uncharted territory.

The rebalancing of economic growth and the rising economic power of emerging markets, together with profound demographic changes such as the rise of the new middle class and an aging population, will define who and where the next generation of banking customers are, and what products and services they need. Meeting new needs for new customer groups and extending financial access can have a huge social dividend, but this implies important changes in the way banks will have to operate. These opportunities are already driving exciting innovation to reach and serve customers in many emerging markets.

Technological change has ushered in an era of digital revolution. The rapid adoption of technology by consumers is accelerating changes in both expectations and behavior. Meanwhile, new technological capabilities are enabling banks to reach customers in new ways, achieve new levels of efficiency, or reach new levels of insight. And as these changes benefit incumbents, digital innovation in particular, makes many traditional markets more contestable, ushering in a new era of competition. As we approach the first time in history where nearly everyone is connected, this will be a crucial dynamic of change.

At the same time, banks are subject to new requirements for transparency and governance, designed to rebuild the trust that has been severely challenged with customers and the public. As a key currency for banking, trust is critical. The very legitimacy of the banking sector as special economic agents is challenged. Alternative forms of financial intermediation, from shadow banking to peer-to-peer banking, are maturing at the same time that the structure and activities of traditional banks are under scrutiny. Banks will need to chart a course that allows them to maintain their key economic role.

Each of these changes, in itself, represents a huge challenge and opportunity for banks. Together they signify new rules of the game, new ways of doing business, and a new competitive landscape. However, the real challenge lies in the complex and compound nature of these changes which create strategic paradoxes. Banks will need to clearly assess their own landscape and choose which course to navigate.

The new landscape is not a static environment. We are all operating in a more uncertain and volatile world. For banks, future high performance will demand new capabilities and new principles that allow management to face these changes with greater agility. The leaders of banks today have a unique opportunity to remake their institutions for the future. There will be winners and losers. The journey starts with a clear appraisal of the new landscape.

INTRODUCTION

Landscape After the Battle

The world was already undergoing major economic, geopolitical, and technological change before the preliminary phase of the Great Recession started in the summer of 2007. The rise of emerging economies, the growing financial imbalances across countries, population aging, and the dawn of the age of mobile telecommunications were already on everybody's mind. When Lehman Brothers Holdings Inc., collapsed the world held its breath. A new era in financial services was ushered in as people realized that the twentieth century had come to an end in more ways than one.

The financial sector in general, and banks in particular, will never be the same. The crisis made readily apparent some of the most important contradictions in traditional banking models. Everything from customer relationships and distribution channels to sources of income, and from leverage and capital levels to talent management, became the subject of fierce debate among bankers, regulators, policymakers, and the general public. Collectively, banks saw their most important asset, the public's trust, vanish even faster than their capital ratios were eroded by the onslaught of the crisis. It seemed as if the way of doing banking that had characterized the previous three decades was coming to an end. The realization was, and continues to be, that a new banking business model is sorely needed. While the crisis did not affect emerging economies due to their lesser integration in global capital markets, banks in Latin America and Asia will also be affected by the broader demographic and technological changes. Many of them will be in a position to capitalize on the growth of their respective domestic market, and some may successfully expand overseas.

A New Era in Banking: The Landscape After the Battle identifies the main drivers of change at the heart of this wholesale transformation of the financial services industry. We dissect demographic, economic, regulatory, and technological change in order to assess the consequences for banking business models. We will examine the strengths of the emerging players in the field, and also address what incumbent financial institutions have to do if they are to survive in the new landscape. Our analysis seeks to untangle the severe mutations that have taken place in the banking sector, and to contextualize them within broader trends that go well beyond the strict confines of the crisis. Banks are more vulnerable than ever to the crosscurrents of economic, demographic, regulatory, and technological change. The crisis merely revealed an industry structure that was very fragile and subject to systemic disruption.

THE GATHERING STORM

We begin by outlining the most proximate and immediate factors that contributed to the perfect storm of 2008. They mostly have to do with two assumptions that pervaded thinking about financial services and financial markets. The first was that markets can and do function efficiently, seamlessly ensuring the allocation of capital so as to benefit the overall economy and society. The second had to do with the belief that the financial sector could not only regulate itself effectively, but also that the system's efficiency and normal functioning required extensive governmental deregulation. These assumptions brought about a series of mind-sets among bankers, investors, and regulators that proved fatal during the unfolding of the crisis, including the blind belief in the irreversibility of the new era of the "Great Moderation," the neglect of rising financial imbalances, and the staggering complexity and interdependencies between the financial sector and public finances.

Confidence in the Continuity of the Great Moderation

The crisis was preceded by a phase of widespread complacency regarding the fundamental health of the financial system and the economy as a whole. Known as the "Great Moderation," the period stretching from the turn of the twenty-first century to 2007 gave birth to large macroeconomic imbalances, rising financial globalization, and a relaxation of risk-assessment practices by financial institutions. Thanks to a booming global economy and lax monetary policies, Europe and the United States witnessed an extraordinary period of growth in private and public financial leverage, with debt levels among banks, companies, households, and governments escalating relentlessly.

Expanding Global Imbalances

In part as a reaction to the East Asian, Brazilian, and Russian episodes of financial distress during the late 1990s, emerging economies focused much of their policymaking on the goal of amassing large amounts of foreign-exchange reserves. By exporting cheap manufactured goods or natural resources, these economies generated large surpluses in their current account, with most of them becoming net capital exporters. At the same time, several European countries and the United States went more deeply into deficit, putting pressure on exchange rates and creating the conditions for financial bubbles in the deficit countries.

Most importantly, large surpluses led to both the widening and deepening of financial markets as the deficit countries relied on international credit to keep their economies going. Interest rates were at historically low levels, and lenders were so awash in capital that they placed no restrictions on the amounts that borrowing countries and their governments could get. The entire global financial system was counting on continued growth based on increasing capital flows from the surplus to the deficit economies.

The role of the emerging economies in the global financial landscape was transformed. They became the lenders of last resort, counting on the developed markets of Europe and especially the United States as the consumers of last resort. In parallel, little attention was paid to the likely future evolution of the dollar, the world's leading reserve currency, and the viability of the euro, the world's second. While the band played on, economic and financial actors turned their heads away from the fundamental weaknesses and potential pitfalls embedded in the global financial architecture.

Expansion of Financial Systems

The financial system grew in size and complexity during the era of the Great Moderation, rising global financial imbalances, and lax monetary policy. The U.S. financial sector, for instance, came to account for nearly 20 percent of all economic activity, and more than 40 percent of total corporate profits. The counterpart to this trend was the increase in public and private indebtedness, with bank balance sheets expanding considerably. Credit was plentiful, and nobody seemed to care about the long-term ability of borrowers to pay back loans as long as the machine for making them kept on working. In many countries, a large chunk of the financing had to do with real estate assets or with financial instruments whose value depended on such assets.

The Credit Crunch

A realization that the party could not go on forever started in the summer of 2007 with the collapse of the interbank lending market in several European economies, triggered by the first signs of trouble in the U.S. subprime mortgage market. The chain reaction was swift and reached most high-income economies in a matter of months. The ensuing credit crunch brought the real estate sector and the financial system to the brink of collapse before it started to cause trouble among nonfinancial firms, which put on hold investment plans, sending the real economy into a downward spiral.

Unconventional Measures by the Central Banks

The growing emergency was met first and foremost by the decisive and quite extraordinary actions by central banks, which provided liquidity on a scale never seen before. Monetary authorities saved the global financial system from utter collapse by acting in a coordinated way, thus averting a much deeper crisis that could have been comparable to that of the 1930s.

Diabolic Loop Between Banks and Treasuries

With the real economy in a tailspin, the next victims of the crisis were governments themselves. Already highly leveraged, they saw their annual deficits soar as tax revenue plummeted and unemployment grew. The crisis had mutated into a full-blown sovereign debt debacle. A rather intractable "diabolic loop" between banks and treasuries developed in Europe because, unlike in Japan, most public debt was on the balance sheets of financial institutions. Investors quickly grasped the situation and fled from the bond markets in Europe's periphery, in spite of the high interest rates that the deficit countries had to pay in order to roll over their debt. The European Central Bank had to step in vigorously to purchase peripheral government debt in order to avoid the end of the common currency. The Federal Reserve intervened earlier and even more aggressively by purchasing trillions of dollars of government debt in order to provide a stimulus to the economy that was impossible to provide on the fiscal side.

Complexity and Interdependence

The crisis made it readily apparent that large, highly leveraged, and interlinked financial institutions were vulnerable. Big problems in one division of a bank had the potential to bring down the whole. The blurring of investment and commercial banking left deposit-taking institutions subject to enormous risks that conventional models had grossly underestimated. Adding to the problem was the fact that large banks with sprawling global operations fell under several supervisory regimes, often engaged in regulatory arbitrage, and found ways to game the system that undermined its stability.

Risk Management, Shadow Banking, and Scandals

The banking sector was also rife with insufficient or ineffective risk-management systems, a problem exacerbated by banks' high degree of financial leverage. At the same time, "shadow banking" practices in credit intermediation and maturity transformation led to the multiplication of systemic risks. Fraudulent management added to the woes of bad management, compounding the problem and making it more difficult for supervisors to do their jobs. These issues also hastened the decline in the reputation of financial institutions and trust in their solidity and stability.

Links Between Financial Dynamics and the Real Economy

Arguably, the crisis has been most severe in Europe; this is because of the prominent role that banks play in the financing of economic activity and because of the rigidity of the labor market, which makes adjustment much slower and ultimately more painful. Politicians failed to grasp the importance of providing swift solutions to the deterioration of bank balance sheets before the problem infected the rest of the economy.

Distrust in the Banks

The banks, as key institutions in the financial system, are both the perpetrators and victims of the crisis and the way it was handled. The importance and efficiency of bank intermediation has been called into question, providing fertile soil for new experimentation. Banks lost goodwill among customers, policymakers, and regulators. Many have come to perceive banks not as institutions that manage risks but as entities that create or amplify them. Remuneration practices have accordingly come under fierce attack given the broken link between performance and prudence, on the one hand, and compensation, on the other.

Reconsidering of the Role of Banks

The question of the "social utility" of banking has come to the fore, coined by Lord Turner, then chairman of the Financial Services Authority (FSA), given the broad economic and social impacts of the banking crisis. Political, regulatory, and stakeholder pressures have led to a shift in the balance of power away from an agenda primarily focused on the creation of shareholder value toward a more explicit social agenda. This shift has manifested itself in many ways, including an increased focus on consumer protection and transparency, political pressure to focus on economic outcomes such as maintaining credit to lenders and households, and increasing focus on financial inclusion activities.

However, at the root, there is recognition that, given the central economic and social role of banks, an excessive focus on shareholder outcomes can lead to or worsen existing areas of market failure. While regulators and the banking industry will dismantle many barriers to entry that have resulted in oligopolistic banking markets—such as ownership of payments infrastructure or bank market entry requirements—a more fundamental shift in bank governance must embrace a stakeholder value model as well as shareholder returns.

Demographic Shifts and New Technology

The crisis also brought to the fore two long-standing trends that banks were slow to respond to. The first was a pincer movement involving shifting demographics and technology that put retail banks at risk of losing touch with their customers. On the one hand, continued aging of the population requires a rethinking of product portfolios; on the other, the coming of age of the millennial generation and the pervasiveness of mobile telecommunications technology undermines the traditional branch-based model of banking.

The trouble for banks is that these trends and events require them to simultaneously return to traditional banking models and to address the new challenges posed by technology and shifting demographics. Many banks will need to refocus on the "boring banking" activities associated with the retail business, under conditions of increased regulation, higher capital requirements, and enhanced supervision. At the same time, banks will need to cope with the wave of financial innovations introduced by nonbank financial intermediaries, which include private equity funds, hedge funds, sovereign wealth funds, electronic payment service providers, and crowdfunding sites among others.

DRIVING TOWARD A NEW BUSINESS MODEL FOR BANKS

Banks will, in general, face a new competitive environment characterized by downward pressure on margins, a crowded field with perhaps too many intermediaries, and customer demands for differentiation. These forces might invite industry consolidation, but megabanks will continue to draw the attention from regulators and the public amid calls to avoid situations of "too big to fail" and "too complex or interconnected to fail." These conflicting forces and demands will surely make the job of banks much more complicated and subject to criticism. General animosity toward the world of banking and finance is unlikely to subside anytime soon.

In the chapters that follow we provide analytical insight into the complex mass of trends and events affecting the banking sector. We will highlight the connections among them and show that addressing one factor in isolation is unlikely to provide a solid foundation of sustainable profitability for the banking sector as a whole. We dedicate a chapter each: to the issues of global macro trends affecting banking, the trend toward greater regulation, the new competitive dynamics in a fundamentally reshaped industry, the erosion of legitimacy and trust, and the challenge and opportunities in the area of digital banking. In the last chapter, we take stock of these changes and formulate the foundations and organizing principles of a new business model for banks, linking our recommendations to the trends identified in chapter 1.

CHAPTER 1

Macro Trends

The global financial crisis that started in 2007 and reached its climax in the fall of 2008 certainly demarcates a before and an after in the global banking landscape. In developed markets, hundreds of banks worldwide went bust, and virtually every financial institution was affected in one way or another. Many had to accept government aid or bailouts. Many bank employees lost their jobs, and many customers saw their savings or their investments dwindle.

However, it would be inaccurate to assume that the fallout from the crisis is the only relevant, or even the most important, factor reshaping the industry at the present time. The transition from the twentieth to the twenty-first century has brought to the fore a number of other changes with fundamental implications for the way in which banks do business. The landscape after the battle is exceedingly complex and mired in uncertainty. Banks have not faced such a difficult predicament in decades.

Figure 1-1 summarizes the key factors affecting banking at the present time and into the near future. In this chapter we will deal with macro trends affecting banking, including changing demographics, global patterns of economic activity, and emerging technology. In subsequent chapters we will analyze the shifting regulatory

Figure 1-1. Key Trends Affecting Banking

Source: Afi, Analistas Financieros Internacionales, S.A.

climate, which includes new requirements as to capital adequacy, separation of different types of banking activities, risk management, consumer protections, and taxation. We will also scrutinize changes in competitive dynamics due to excess capacity, disintermediation, and the war for talent. Finally, we will gauge the impact of the banking industry's loss of legitimacy, lack of trust, criticism about bankers' compensation, and eroding customer loyalty.

The four key demographic, economic, and technological macro trends we have identified are transforming the banking landscape in game-changing ways. The first has to do with population aging, which is altering market dynamics not only in developed countries but in emerging economies as well, ushering in both a large generation of retirees and a new, brave generation of young millennials. The second is the phenomenal growth of emerging economies, which have come to account for more than half of global economic activity, and whose financial sectors are expanding fast as well. The third is the rise of the global middle class of consumers, driven by the increasing importance of the emerging world. And the fourth is the revolution in connectivity and mobility enabled by new technology.

POPULATION AGING

One way of thinking about the role of finance in the modern economy is to consider the effect of the life cycle on the behavior of individuals and families. Savings and consumption behavior change dramatically as people go through the different stages of the life cycle. In the contemporary world, we have come to think of life as a succession of discrete phases from childhood and adolescence to youth, maturity, and old age. Over time, people devote their time to different activities such as study, work, and leisurely retirement. As a result, the demand for credit, investment, and other types of financial services shifts over the life cycle. Depending on the size of the different age cohorts, the banking sector will experience a shift as well. In rapidly aging countries, banking services tailored to the older age groups will become proportionally more important. In countries with high fertility rates, the reverse will be true, at least for the next two or three decades.

The contemporary banking sector has never dealt with a situation in which an increasing proportion of the population is above the age of fifty. Several countries will very soon have more grandparents than grandchildren. This is due to the rapid decrease in birth rates and the continuing increase in life expectancy. People are living twenty-five years longer on average than they were in 1950, and they are having fewer children.

For the next three or four decades, populations in Europe, North

America, East Asia (including China), and even India will age. According to the United Nations Population Division's medium data, in the year 2000 Germany and Italy had more people age sixty and above than people below age twenty. By 2010 Japan, Greece, Portugal, Spain, Austria, Bulgaria, Slovenia, Croatia, Finland, Switzerland, and Sweden were in the same situation. By 2025, forty-six countries or territories are projected to have more old people than young people. China and Russia will join the trend by 2030, the United States by 2035, Brazil by 2040, Mexico and Indonesia by 2050, and India by 2070.

The size of the population age sixty-five and over is projected to triple by 2050 to 1.5 billion, and it will represent 16 percent of the world's total. Much of this growth will take place not in Europe and North America but in the emerging world, especially East Asia (China, Japan, and South Korea), where one billion people age sixty-five or older will live by 2050. Thus, it is important to note that aging affects both developed and emerging economies (see Table 1-1).

The impact of population aging on banking is mainly driven by the fact that most financial wealth is held by people above the age of fifty. Thus, early in the process of population aging, asset accumulation and savings increase, as middle-aged people set money aside for retirement. Within ten or fifteen years, however, people start deaccumulating assets and using savings as they go into retirement. In addition, it is important to keep in mind that risk aversion tends to increase with age. What are the implications of population aging for banking? Let us sketch out the most important consequences:

• Demand for mortgages and consumer credit will slow down and even decline as the population ages, while demand for products that allow people to diversify risks or that enable wealth decumulation (e.g., reverse mortgages) will grow. Banks can protect themselves against this trend by enrolling new customers or by diversifying into markets with younger populations.

Table 1-1. Global Population, by Age and Gender

	Total Age 15–29		Total Age 65+		Women Age 65+
	Billion	% of total	Billion	% of total	Billion
World 2010	2.29	33.1	0.53	7.7	0.30
World 2020	2.39	31.0	0.72	9.3	0.39
World 2030	2.44	29.0	0.97	11.6	0.53
World 2040	2.57	28.4	1.25	13.9	0.68
World 2050	2.60	27.3	1.49	15.6	0.81
Developed 2010	0.33	26.7	0.20	16.1	0.12
Developed 2020	0.31	24.0	0.24	19.1	0.14
Developed 2030	0.29	22.6	0.29	22.5	0.17
Developed 2040	0.30	23.0	0.32	24.6	0.18
Developed 2050	0.29	22.6	0.33	25.8	0.19
Emerging 2010	1.66	34.4	0.30	6.2	0.16
Emerging 2020	1.71	31.8	0.43	8.0	0.23
Emerging 2030	1.70	29.1	0.63	10.7	0.34
Emerging 2040	1.74	28.2	0.85	13.7	0.46
Emerging 2050	1.71	26.6	1.03	16.0	0.55
Least developed 2010	0.29	34.7	0.03	3.5	0.02
Least developed 2020	0.37	35.1	0.04	3.7	0.02
Least developed 2030	0.45	34.8	0.06	4.4	0.03
Least developed 2040	0.52	33.9	0.08	5.4	0.05
Least developed 2050	0.60	32.9	0.10	6.9	0.07

Source: United Nations Population Division, *World Population Prospects 2012*

• Demand for bundled products will increase—for example, annuities combined with life insurance—especially if they enable the customer to diversify risks. The trend toward less risky investments may also have a negative impact on long-term economic and financial growth.

• Some customers will relocate geographically at least once during their retirement, first toward leisure destinations and later closer to their families. These movements will force banks to rethink their distribution channel strategy and the principle of geographic proximity to the customer. In some cases, cross-border distribution of financial services to retirees will be needed, either by the bank directly or through alliances with other banks.

• Instead of profiting from traditional intermediation, banks will find more opportunities to increase noninterest income, including advisory services, asset management, and annuities, among others.

• A declining savings rate in economies with substantial populations of retirees may force banks to tap into more expensive sources of funds, with implications for profitability, capital adequacy ratios, and the overall stability of the financial system.

• Geographic diversification of banks across countries with different demographic profiles will become an effective way of cushioning the impact of population aging, contributing to banks' desire to engage in cross-border acquisitions.

• The growing trend of customers in advanced markets toward self-provision for retirement, health, and education, represents a potentially large opportunity for banks. This shift is driven in part by the uncertainties surrounding government provision of such services. It allows banks to engage with mass-market advice for private savings, investment, and pension provision.

Financial Decision Making over the Life Cycle

A relevant aspect of the rebalancing of populations by age group as a result of declining fertility and increasing life expectancy has to do with financial behavior and planning. Young people and old people are more likely to make mistakes when it comes to financial decisions than middle-aged people, for different reasons. Young people lack the experience, and old people may start to decline cognitively. There is some evidence that networking may help overcome such limitations in both age groups, with important implications for the way in which banks relate to their customers and help them make sound decisions. For young people, social networking sites can be used to help them see how their peers make decisions. For retirees, face-to-face interaction and social activities may become important ways to help them make better decisions.[1] The rise of online portfolio relationship management (PRM) may alter some of these assumptions, especially if they incorporate social platforms.

Banks should expect more regulation as a result of population aging. Some of the new regulatory areas under consideration include enhancing rules about the disclosure of terms, imposing new fiduciary duties on sales agents, and establishing a system for ex ante financial product approval.[2]

Gender Effects

Another important demographic aspect related to aging to keep in mind is the gender gap in life expectancy. The average woman in the developed world is currently expected to live for eighty-one years and the average man for seventy-four years. The longevity gap between women and men means that the older segments of the population are predominantly female (see Table 1-1). This fact has important implications for banks. Women have different financial needs than men, especially if they were not the main earners in the household.

Most importantly, women have different attitudes toward money and personal finance. They are more concerned than men about having enough money for retirement (remember, they live longer), for taking care of children and parents, and for education. They tend to be less competitive when it comes to making investment choices, and they obtain lower scores on standardized financial literacy tests than men,[3] although this is likely to change now that, in many countries, women outnumber and outperform men at all levels of education. Women are also accumulating more wealth than in the past, thanks to their vastly expanded labor-market opportunities. In the

U.S., 37 percent of all high-net-worth individuals (i.e., millionaires) are women. Japan is another country with a high proportion, 31 percent. The global average is about 27 percent, in Europe and Latin America it is 18 percent and in the Middle East 14 percent.[4] Some banks are starting to offer differentiated products and platforms for women, especially in the area of wealth advisory.

Lifestyle Shifts

Changing role models, cultural expectations, and demographic trends will continue to affect household size and composition, with important implications for banks. In both advanced and emerging markets, people are waiting longer to establish a household, studying longer, and returning to school after their first job. The number of one-person households is growing, as is the number of households with a divorced parent. In many cases, couples are keeping their finances separate while living together. These new types of living and financial arrangements result in a wide variety of new financial needs that are not currently served by traditional banks.

Aging and the Stock Market

Banks will also need to watch the effects of demographics on financial markets more broadly. A recent study demonstrated that population aging exerts downward pressure on stock prices, controlling for a large number of other conflating factors. Individual investors reallocate their portfolios away from equities as they approach retirement. Once in retirement, they purchase annuities or simply spend their savings. An economy with a large population of older people is less dynamic, also dampening stock prices.[5]

It is clear that population aging will affect all aspects of banking, including the structure of assets and liabilities, balance-sheet strength, growth strategies, distribution channel mix, and skill requirements for personnel. It is important to note that the effects of population aging on national savings and the ability of deposit-taking banks to meet capital adequacy ratios may prompt new regulations. In sum, population aging creates a very different scenario for banks, one that will last for at least thirty or forty years, until old-age mortality rebalances the population age pyramid or fertility trends start changing again.

In sum, banks face a much changed demographic landscape in which they will have to focus on winning over young customers and transforming their way of doing business to accommodate a large number of people in retirement and living longer than ever. The growing importance of women as financial decision makers in both developed and developing countries will also invite banks to rethink their product and distribution strategies. These are the most important direct effects of current population trends. The indirect effects will also be enormously consequential as patterns of economic growth, aggregate savings, and financial market development shift in the wake of demographic change.

THE GROWTH OF EMERGING MARKETS

The phenomenal growth of the emerging markets of Asia, Latin America, the Middle East, and Africa during the past two decades has transformed the global economy, creating new production hubs, consumer markets, credit markets, and, especially, new patterns of financial flows and wealth accumulation. These changes are so pervasive and massive in scale that it is hard to underestimate the extent to which they will affect the banking industry.

A first important trend has to do with the increase in the size of the banking market. Consumers and small firms are notoriously underbanked in emerging economies. Experts agree that the rate of growth of financial and banking services will be faster than the growth of the economy over the next two or three decades. In particular, credit will expand quickly in emerging economies, and these could well become a greater market than the G7 economies.

Bank credit will increase especially quickly because of underbanking and underdevelopment of capital markets in emerging economies. Most experts predict that, at least initially, emerging economies will resemble Europe more than the United States in terms of the strong presence of banks and bank credit in the economy. In other words, banks with experience in European markets will be in principle better prepared to operate in emerging economies.

Emerging-market growth is likely to be driven by international trade. In fact, exports and imports are growing faster than GDP, and in some cases ahead of credit markets. This will represent an additional opportunity for banks, especially those already familiar with the wholesale and private aspects of trade financing.

The growth of emerging economies also means that individual and family wealth will accumulate more quickly there than in Europe and the United States. One study predicts investable wealth accumulation will grow at a cumulative annual rate of 9.8 percent in the Asia-Pacific region and 6.8 percent in the Middle East until 2015 compared with 6.2 percent in Europe and 5.7 percent in North America.[6] Higher wealth growth in emerging economies is driven by overall economic expansion, an increasingly uneven distribution of income, and the first-mover advantages that many business owners and entrepreneurs enjoy in emerging markets. Banks with the ability to grow in emerging markets stand to benefit from this trend.

Secondly, the rise of banking in emerging economies will accelerate the trend toward the internationalization of banks, for two reasons. Emerging-market banks will seek to establish a base in developed markets as a way to access capital markets, and to tap into knowledge and expertise. Emerging-market banks will need to follow their customers, especially wealthy individuals and small businesses, to developed markets. Some of that expansion will take the form of establishing representative and wholesale operations, but mergers and acquisitions are also likely to increase. The second reason is that growth in emerging markets will attract new entrants, especially from stagnating developed markets. North American and European banks have already set their eyes on opportunities in emerging markets, attracted by their growth prospects and by the possibility of further diversifying their footprint across demographic and monetary regimes.

Developed-market banks face important dilemmas when strategizing about emerging markets:

- Can a large bank afford not to have a retail presence in emerging markets?
- Will business customers demand a presence in emerging markets?
- Can banks learn from emerging markets without having a presence in them?

Ultimately, the response of banks to the growth of emerging economies will involve difficult tradeoffs in terms of the allocation of resources across markets—including both balance-sheet strength and managerial attention. Banks find themselves at a crossroads precisely at a time when their strength and margin for action are substantially reduced as a result of the global financial crisis.

A final aspect to keep in mind regarding financial services and banking in emerging markets is that future growth is highly dependent on a sustained improvement in women's labor market opportunities and gender equality. Due to a combination of legal discrimination, traditions, and social norms, women in developing and emerging economies are less likely to own a bank account or to use savings and credit products.[7]

THE RISE OF THE GLOBAL MIDDLE CLASS

One of the most fundamental game-changing trends of the last two decades has to do with the expansion of consumer markets in emerging economies. The rise of the global middle class is driven by economic growth and new economic opportunities in the large emerging economies, especially China, India, Brazil, Indonesia, Turkey, and Mexico. The Organisation for Economic Co-operation and Development (OECD) estimates that in 2022 the number of middle-class people will exceed the number of poor people for the first time in human history. The middle class has been defined by the OECD as individuals with at least US $10 to spend per day but less than US $100. Most importantly, while in 2014 two-thirds of the global middle class lived in Europe and the United States, by the year 2022 two-thirds will live in emerging economies. China and India will account for nearly half of all middle-class consumers.[8] Interestingly, India will have the world's largest middle class by 2040, because it will have an overall population larger than China's and a more equitable distribution of income.

The statistics about the growing middle class are even more impressive when looking at their purchasing power. Over the next two decades about $34 trillion worth of new middle-class purchasing power will be created, increasing to a total of nearly $56 trillion globally. Most of the growth will take place in the Asia-Pacific (see Table 1-2). No bank can afford to ignore this trend.

Retail banking markets will expand in unison with the rise of the global middle class. People enjoying increasing incomes need all manner of financial services, including deposit accounts, savings

Table 1-2. Middle-Class Consumption (Trillion 2005 Dollars)

	2010	2030
World	21.3	55.7
North America	5.6	5.8
Europe	8.1	11.3
Central & South America	1.5	3.1
Asia Pacific	4.9	32.6
Sub-Saharan Africa	0.3	0.8
Middle East and North Africa	0.8	2.0

Source: Homi Kharas, *The Emerging Middle Class in Developing Countries* (OECD, 2010)

products, mortgages, consumer credit, and so on. The middle class accounts for the bulk of purchases of durable goods, including automobiles, household appliances, and consumer electronics. The middle class has an aspiration for social mobility, and this generally translates into attaching huge importance to education and to stability. This means that education loans, pension funds, and insurance will be in high demand in the most rapidly growing emerging economies. Banks can profitably address middle-class financial needs as they unfold, from consumer credit and savings to credit cards, mortgages, and insurance.

It is also key to consider middle-class consumer behavior in terms of its pronounced brand orientation and the value placed on commitment and loyalty. In advanced markets, banks will need to undo the damage caused by the financial crisis in terms of their reputation. The public has lost much trust in banks, and this has affected their brand image. Banks without a strong corporate identity and attractive brand will find it difficult to fight for market share among global middle-class consumers. The key idea here is to offer differentiation on the scale needed to serve the large emerging middle-class markets, that is, a mass-premium strategy emphasizing a certain degree of exclusivity within an affordable price range.

TECHNOLOGY

Banking is an ancient art, but one which has evolved to take advantage of new innovations. Technology, especially in the area of telecommunications and information access, played a key role from the early years, as bankers could gain an advantage by being the first to learn about relevant news and events. Famously, Nathan Rothschild's network of agents and couriers enabled him to learn about Wellington's victory at Waterloo in 1815 a full day ahead of the government, which provided him with an advantage in trading bonds. For the last half century, banks have made huge investments in technology in order to make their back-office operations more efficient, take advantage of arbitrage opportunities in different markets, and meet customer needs and demands.

From the ATM to the Internet, new banking technologies have been aimed at enhancing convenience, reducing branch visits, increasing transaction speed, and reducing costs. At the turn of the twenty-first century, the main areas for technology adoption in banking include:

• **Mobility.** The widespread adoption of mobile phones and, increasingly, smartphones poses a challenge for banks as they revisit their distribution strategy in the wake of the global financial crisis. Terms such as "remote deposit capture" and "multichannel experience" are now widely discussed by bankers worldwide.

• **Location-based marketing,** including loyalty programs, special offers targeted to specific needs, and other types of real-time initiatives.

• **Interactive customer experience,** across multiple channels and platforms, creating seamless interactions. This trend is key to the competitiveness of banks in both mature and emerging markets, and is essential to attract customers who are young and technologically savvy.

• **Integrated payment systems, electronic wallets, and other money-moving technologies,** which enable people to seamlessly make and receive payments, and to hold digital cash. This trend represents a major threat to banks in terms of disintermediation.

• **Digital social networks, peer comparisons, and other related technologies for socially based banking,** which may be useful for both back-office and bank-customer interaction. Banks may be able to optimize customer screening, loan approval, and similar processes with the help of new technology, but they will also need to invest heavily in new technological capabilities that offer customers real-time, cheap, and reliable digital financial services.

• **Banking available everywhere 24/7,** virtually and literally at the customer's fingertips.

• **The end, potentially, of back-office systems,** as banks move toward hosted and cloud-based systems. The tradeoff between cost and flexibility will need to be revisited. Most importantly, established banks will need to reassess the threat posed by new, nimbler competitors with a lower fixed-cost structure thanks to new computing models.

• **Big-data analytics,** or the immense possibilities for developing and targeting new products for specific types of customers and even situations.

Technology and Generational Effects

A very important aspect of new technology adoption by banks has to do with the so-called millennial generation (those born between 1980 and 1999), who have grown up in a world in which e-mail, texting, multiplayer games, and digital social media are pervasive. In the United States, 75 percent of millennials have a profile on a social networking site (compared with 30 percent among the baby boomers and 50 percent among generation X). Only 20 percent of millennials believe that owning a home is a very important thing to accomplish in life, and about 15 percent agree that having a high-paying career is. Technology is what defines them: 83 percent place their mobile phone right next to their beds while sleeping, compared to 68 percent for generation X and 50 percent for baby boomers. Women tend to score several percentage points higher on each of these characteristics and behaviors than men (except for posting a video of themselves online), and those with a college education score even higher.[9]

As the bank customers of the future, the expectations of millennials are radically different from those of their parents and grandparents, and they will be hard to satisfy. At the present time, banks are not perceived by the millennial generation as cool. There is a yawning gap between what banks offer and what the millennial generation expects when it comes to financial services. Young people want to be connected, engaged, thrilled, and excited. They like technological disruption if it brings them convenience, expanded choice, and image. If anything, most retail banks have attempted over the last few decades to be traditional and unexciting, with the notable exceptions of Frank by OCBC, SuperFlash by Intesa Sanpaolo, Alior Sync, and Hello bank!, among others. In general, millennials are not as interested as their parents and grandparents in mortgages and automobile loans, mainly because they are not as keen on becoming homeowners and they prefer to use other means of transportation.

Strategic Considerations in New Technology

Banks will need to pay attention to several key issues when it comes to adopting new technology:

- How can technology be used to attract young customers and retain retirees?
- How can banks avoid the widespread perception that they are constantly behind the curve in terms of new technology, especially in the age of mobility, cloud computing, and wearable devices?
- Can banks deploy technology to develop further sources of income in addition to interest and fees, especially in terms of loyalty, convenience, advisory services, and the like?

- How can trust, privacy, and security be enhanced?
- How should the banking workforce of the future be trained and motivated in order to take advantage of new technologies?

Banks will need to reconsider which transactions are routine and which are not. A key element is deciding which transactions may be stepping-stones into sales of additional products and which are purely spot interactions with the customer. Technology needs to be used in different ways depending on the nature of the transaction. And above all, banks need to incorporate technology in a way that does not commoditize their business. They must avoid competing on the basis of price alone.

A major challenge will be to reallocate spending on IT away from maintaining legacy systems and into the new technologies of cloud computing, mobile banking, and digital social media. Most banks spend three-quarters or more of their IT budget making sure that their existing systems continue to work seamlessly. In most cases, however, spending just one-fourth on new technological initiatives and systems may not be enough to stay ahead of new competitors and meet customer expectations.

But perhaps the biggest danger will be hubris. Bankers are fond of saying that when the ATMs came along experts predicted the death of the bank branch, and perhaps the death of banks altogether. That, they note, did not happen. With the advent of the Internet, experts again predicted that banks might disappear or at least be transformed. While it is true that a new technology by itself will not necessarily disrupt everything, this time around circumstances seem to be conspiring to erode the traditional business model of banks:

- In the advanced markets, the financial crisis has put banks on the defensive in the court of public opinion and in the minds of regulators.

- Young people, who are banks' future customers, distrust banks and do not understand why they need one if they have a smartphone filled with financial and payments apps.
- Much of the future growth in financial services will occur in emerging markets, where banks have traditionally been less pervasive than they are in developed markets.
- Large companies with large volumes of transactions would like to get a slice of the pie when it comes to offering financial and payments services; these companies include utilities, large retailers, and airline companies, among others.

Considering future scenarios is one way to set the stage for the discussion in subsequent chapters of what banks may do in order to cope with the challenges, and benefit from the opportunities, created by new technologies. Some of the most revolutionary possibilities include:

- A world in which a widely available peer-to-peer platform enables individuals and small businesses to obtain credit and make deposits, or to secure any other type of financial service, without the intervention of a financial intermediary.

- A world in which new technology enables nonbank competitors—telecommunications companies, big retailers, etc.—to launch a wide variety of financial products and services.

- A world in which banks reinvent themselves and occupy a central position in a transformed financial services industry in which virtual and brick-and-mortar components offer customers a seamless experience.

These scenarios are not mutually exclusive. In fact, the future will not be determined only by technology. The strategies and actions of key competitors in the banking industry and in other industries will shape the evolution of financial services over the next two to three decades.

CONCLUSION

To summarize, in the new competitive scenario after the crisis, banks are facing a number of key challenges:

- A redistribution of their customer base by age and by gender.
- Maturing markets in developed countries, and rapid growth in under-banked countries where banks may not become the most important financial institutions.
- A rising number of middle-class consumers who are aspirational, brand oriented, and status seeking.
- A millennial generation of young people who are skeptical about traditional banks and banking practices, if not hostile to them.
- A host of new technologies with important implications for back-office operations, distribution channels, customer interaction, and, more broadly, the entire way of doing business as a financial intermediary.

The confluence of demographic, economic, financial, and technological trends poses distinct challenges for banks. Their business model and strategies have been rendered at least partially obsolete, especially with the changes in regulation and competitive dynamics stemming from the global financial crisis, the topic of the next chapter.

CHAPTER 2

Regulation

Perhaps the most debated area of financial services that people associate with the global financial crisis, the one that triggered the Great Recession of 2008-2009, is regulatory failure. Public opinion, politicians, and some policy makers have converged on the need to overhaul the financial regulatory system because of its failure to prevent the deepest and widest banking crisis since the 1930s. Although regulatory reform is unlikely to be entirely comprehensive around the world, it is no exaggeration to argue that, in terms of unifying and strengthening global banking regulation, the crisis marks a watershed.

REGULATION IN BANKING: A COMPLETE OVERHAUL

Regulation lies at the heart of the banking business because it has a large impact on levels of risk, growth, and profitability. Moreover, regulation defines the social contract between the banking system and society. Banks enjoy privileges not available to any other sector, mainly in the form of explicit or implicit guarantees from the state that seek to maintain the stability of the financial system in terms of both liquidity and solvency. That special support enjoyed by banks, and some other financial institutions, involves a quid pro quo in which the state exercises comprehensive regulation and supervision. Banks are also expected to provide credit to the rest of the economy, enabling businesses and households to operate.

The crisis has centered the debate on the issue of how far regulation and state guarantees should go without hindering the efficiency of the banking system. Society cannot afford the banking system to fail. The state, however, cannot go as far as guaranteeing that all system units are considered safe. In order to maintain market discipline, it is important for some banks to fail in the normal course of operations and for others to grow. The market needs to be in a position to tell bad banks from good. Thus, regulation needs to strike a balance between stability at the level of the overall banking system, and an effective working of the market mechanism where individual banks enter and exit the system in an orderly way.

The global financial crisis of 2008 put that delicate equilibrium to the test, with heterogeneous outcomes across countries. In the United States and several European countries, not only regulators but also treasuries, as the finance arm of governments, had to intervene in order to shield the system from irreversible damage. The crisis, however, has not erased cross-border differences in terms of the sensitivities and the politics of bank regulation. Another continuing cleavage is the one between macro and micro prudential approaches, which are especially relevant in the case of large, global financial institutions. They operate across different regulatory jurisdictions, while being bound by home country rules in terms of explicit or implicit support, as well as market valuation. As Mervyn King the former governor of the Bank of England famously put it, "Global banks are global in life, but they are local in death."

Regulatory reform, however, should not be seen by banks and other financial institutions as a hindrance. It may well create a huge opportunity for them to differentiate themselves and to rebuild their reputation, especially concerning their privileges, in terms of the willingness of governments to spend trillions of taxpayers' money to avert disaster contrasting with the high levels of compensation at the expense of shareholders and taxpayers.

It is this asymmetry between the distribution of profits and losses from banking activity that spurred tremendous public pressure on politicians to react in terms of more stringent regulation. World leaders read the message from public opinion and embarked on an extremely ambitious agenda of structural reforms, laying the basis for a more sound banking system, one purportedly less likely to be affected by a crisis that has the potential to damage the entire economy.

In practical terms, there are six main areas of regulation with the potential to significantly alter the landscape of the financial services industry:

- **New capital requirements in banking.** As the crisis has demonstrated, the level of capital requirements under the Basel II regulatory regime was clearly insufficient to cover losses in adverse scenarios.

- **New risk-management approaches.** Capital requirements were based on risk measurement metrics (risk-weighted assets) that are somewhat subjective and prone to "manipulation" while offering little value in terms of foreseeing banking failures.

- **Separation of activities.** It is quite generally assumed that large and complex banking organizations enjoy implicit privileges from their "too big to fail" status, as well as perverse incentives to assume excessive risk and place financial stability under severe stress. Structural reforms are under way that will force large banks to clearly separate core intermediation activities, protected by explicit or implicit guarantees, from noncore and risky activities.

- **Incentives.** There is no doubt that excessive risk taking by banks was to a good extent caused by the system of incentives, both at the organizational level and at the level of managers and employees. Compensation policies, especially the heavy reliance on variable bonuses tied to short-term results, constituted an important perverse incentive. This is why one of the key issues in the new regulatory agenda is establishing limits to variable compensation as a proportion of fixed salaries. (Incentives are discussed further in Chapters 3 and 4.)

• **Consumer protection.** Banks have not only been accused of excessive risk taking, but of forgetting about their duties to their customers; there have been several scandals about banks acting in ways that were not in the customer's interest (Libor manipulation, mis-selling of financial products, etc.) which have undermined consumers' trust in banks. Customer protection will be high on any new regulatory agenda, and banks will have to give much more importance in the organization, as well as in the system of incentives, to employees' conduct. Some of the larger banks, especially those most affected by scandals or reputational damages, have established new codes of conduct that are strictly binding for all employees.

• **New taxes on banking and other financial activities.** Banking failures have eaten trillions of taxpayer money across developed countries, while shareholders and managers enjoyed extremely high profits during the boom years. This asymmetry (private benefits versus public losses) is increasing pressures to impose new taxes on banking and financial activities.

Regulatory changes in each of these fields have already been intense and, more importantly, agreed on at an internationally coordinated basis, laying the foundations for a more level playing field in international banking. The goal pursued by international regulators is a reduction in opportunities for regulatory arbitrage. However, the difference between international principles and domestic regulation in the context of national politics and interests[1] means that the path toward a level international playing field will take a long time to achieve.

Banks operating in Europe will be affected by perhaps the most sweeping change in the regulatory structure as a European banking union starts to operate by end 2014. Shifting regulation, supervision, and resolution at the European level will have implications far beyond the countries directly affected. We will analyze these after analyzing the trends in regulation globally.

NEW CAPITAL REQUIREMENTS IN BANKING

Banking is all about managing scarce capital efficiently and profitably. Every stakeholder asks banks to do the best possible job at that. Shareholders are keenly interested in the return on the funds that they provide. Borrowers focus on the cost of credit, as do governments. And regulators care about the sustainability of the banking business over time, especially when the business cycle takes a turn for the worse. The crisis of 2008 brought to the fore long-standing concerns about capital adequacy, and resulted in a widespread perception that, looking down the road, banks would need to be better capitalized in order to forestall future crises or to reduce their impact.

Insufficiency of Former Bank Capital

Simply put, the imposition of minimum capital standards is the cornerstone of banking regulation. And yet, regulators find themselves at a loss when it comes to specifying "safe" or "appropriate" levels of capitalization. Nobody knows how much capital banks should have, but there is no doubt nowadays that they need much more than what has been the rule for the last few decades. This we know because capital levels have proved to be insufficient to perform two basic functions: to cover realized losses and to provide credit to the rest of the economy on an ongoing and sustained basis.

Figure 2-1. Retained Earnings and Equity Offerings Before and After the Crisis (in Billions of U.S. Dollars)

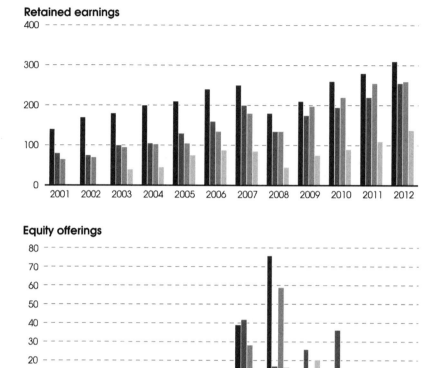

Source: Afi, Analistas Financieros Internacionales, S.A., based on BIS *Annual Report, June 2013*

Nobody knows, with any certainty, the exact amount of bank losses worldwide since the crisis began: different positions in terms of the cycle, and especially different conventions regarding the recognition of losses, make it difficult to compare losses across markets. The IMF estimates overall losses at slightly over 4 percent of total banking assets, with a heterogeneous distributions across geographies. Losses were heavier in the United States and the United Kingdom (in the 5.5 to 7 percent range, when measured over total assets), somewhat smaller in continental Europe (around 3 percent of assets), and markedly lower in Asia (around 1.5 percent of assets).

Given the low level of capital that banks had at the beginning of the crisis, or their high leverage ratios (often exceeding thirty or forty times), it is easy to conclude that overall banking losses have eaten more than 50 percent of capital, and in some cases more than 100 percent. This has happened at the same time that investor appetite for bank capital was virtually nil, leaving shrinking retained earnings and public sector capital injections as the only available sources to replenish capital (see Figure 2-1).

Balance sheet repair has been extremely slow, and clearly insufficient to make banks perform their basic function of providing credit to the economy. In the U.S. and the Eurozone, banks have lowered their lending levels dramatically (see Figures 2-2 and 2-3). The impact on the economy has been more pronounced in the Eurozone given that bank financing plays a much more important role than capital markets.

Figure 2-2. Lending Activity in the Euro Area (Annual Change)

Source: Afi, Analistas Financieros Internacionales, S.A.based on ECB database

Figure 2-3. Lending Activity in the U.S. (Annual Change)

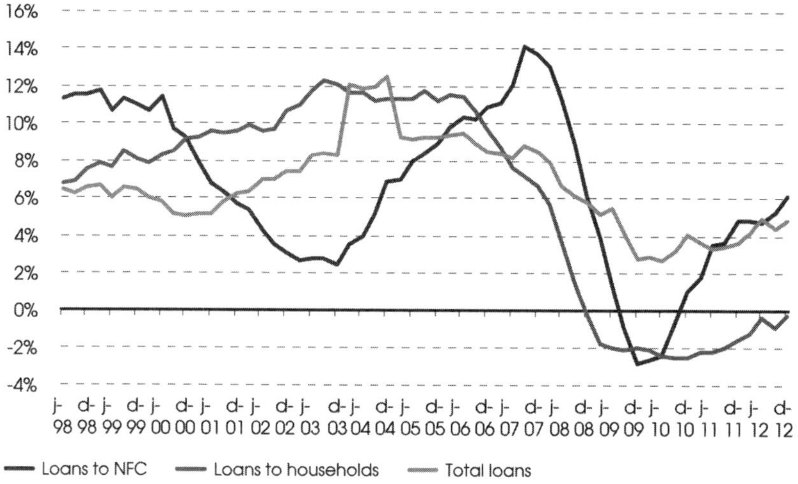

Source: Afi, Analistas Financieros Internacionales, S.A., based on Federal Reserve data

New Capital Requirements

The combination of capital scarcity, the limited ability to raise fresh funds in the markets, and the credit crunch pose a dilemma in terms of new capital requirements. On the one hand, it is clear that banking activity needs far more capital than has been the case in the past; but on the other, raising capital requirements suddenly further jeopardizes bank credit to the real economy. As long as capital requirements are set in terms of a fraction of basic capital over risk-weighted assets, in the absence of easy ways to obtain new capital, higher capital requirements could result in severe cuts in lending as the banks rush to rebalance their capital ratios. For bank regulators, this represents a classic dilemma about time inconsistency: if they are too aggressive today in forcing banks to meet higher capital requirements, they might avoid a future crisis, but they diminish the chances of overcoming the current predicament!

In the context of this dilemma, the Basel III agreement represents a compromise solution. Capital requirements are raised substantially,

Table 2-1. Basel III Capital Requirements

Overview of the Basel III Change on Capital

	Before	After
Minimum common equity requirement	2%	4.5%
+		
Capital conservation buffer met with common equity	0%	2.5%
if under, greater constraints on earning distributions are imposed		
=		
Total common equity requirement	2%	7.0%
+		
Countercyclical buffer	0%	2.5%
According to national circumstances		

Source: European Commission, *High-Level Expert Group on Reforming the Structure of the E.U. Banking Sector*, chaired by Erkki Liikanen, Final Report, Brussels, October 2, 2012

in some cases even doubled (see Table 2-1), but are done so over a long time horizon, which takes the pressure off balance sheets in the short term (see Table 2-2). Such an approach discourages asset dumping as the only available way to rebuild capital ratios, because it allows for the possibility of raising capital once market conditions improve or for retained earnings to increase over time.

Another welcome innovation in the Basel III agreement is the inclusion of liquidity requirements. Two coefficients are defined. The first relates to short-term liquidity and is called Liquidity Coverage Ratio (LCR), which measures the ability to face severe liquidity crises during any one-month period. More important is the second ratio, the Net Stable Funding Ratio (NSFR), which gauges a more balanced financing structure in terms of the stability of the liabilities used to finance long-term assets. Basically, it aims to avoid overreliance on volatile securities, especially those of a short-term nature. These regulatory changes seek to prevent liquidity squeezes, which many see as Basel II's most dramatic failure, as revealed by the collapse of the interbank and wholesale markets during the first year of

Table 2-2. Basel III Phase-In Arrangements (All Dates Are as of January 1)

Phases	2013	2014	2015	2016	2017	2018	2019
Capital							
Leverage ratio						Migration to Pillar 1	
Minimum common equity capital ratio	3.5%	4.0%	4.5% ——————————→				4.5%
Capital conservation buffer					0.625%	1.25%	1.875% 2.5%
Minimum common equity plus capital conservation buffer	3.5%	4.0%	4.5%	5.125%	5.75%	6.375%	7.0%
Phase-in of deductions from CET1		20%	40%	60%	80%	100%	100%
Minimum Tier 1 capital	4.5%	5.5%	6.0% ——————————→				6.0%
Minimum total capital		8.0% ————————————————→					8.0%
Minimum total capital plus conservation buffer		8.0% ————→		8.625%	9.25%	9.875%	10.5%
Capital instruments that no longer qualify as non-core Tier 1 capital or Tier 2 capital	Phased out over 10-year horizon beginning 2013						
Liquidity							
Liquidity coverage ratio – minimum requirement			60%	70%	80%	90%	100%
Net stable funding ratio						Introduce minimum standard	

Source: Basel Committee on Banking Supervision

the crisis. The new ratios, especially the NSFR, attempt to get banks closer to self-sufficiency in terms of the uses and sources of funds with customers.

These additional liquidity requirements, however, are not without implications for funding costs, balance-sheet structure, and increased competition for scarce high-quality assets. This is why, in a similar setting as that applied to capital ratios, the new liquidity requirements will only be binding on a phasing-in period that goes on gradually until 2019.

Implications for the Cost of Capital

A key aspect of the new capital requirements is the potential effect on the cost of capital for banks. This is relevant from a dual perspective.

From the point of view of the banks themselves, the new capital ratios will become the standard in terms of the return on equity, to which bank managers will be bound if they are committed to the principle of value creation for shareholders. From a macroeconomic perspective, the cost of capital for banks is relevant to the extent that it becomes a key reference point for the pricing of loans to companies and households.

It would be misleading to simply recalculate the cost of funding assuming that the cost of equity and the cost of debt will be the same under the new requirements, and therefore the weighted cost of funding will merely reflect the new mix between debt and equity. Such a calculation would increase the overall cost of funding by a considerable amount, as equity is more expensive than debt.

The reason this type of calculation is flawed is that it does not consider the fact that bank equity and debt will be safer with the new capital requirements. In fact, if banks are required to hold more capital, shareholders should be more protected under new capital rules than in the past, and therefore the cost of equity capital should be lower. Such an argument is not only consistent with the classic Modigliani-Miller propositions about indifference between debt and equity, or between dividends and capital gains, but is also clearly seen in banking systems with a long history, like those found in the U.K. and the U.S.

A study by Andrew Haldane,[2] head of financial stability at the Bank of England, offers persuasive evidence. It shows, first, that the extremely low levels of bank capital seen in the last decades were not the long-term historical norm. On the contrary, up until the mid-twentieth century, banks had equity-to-asset ratios closer to 15 or even 20 percent, that is, four or five times higher than in recent decades (see Figure 2-4). Bank ratios were more balanced not only in terms of capital but also in terms of liquid assets to total assets, with ratios five times as high as the norm before the crisis started.

The historical trend became a self-reinforcing dynamic. Increases in bank leverage were simultaneously cause and consequence of the

Figure 2-4. Long-Run Capital-to-Asset Ratios for U.K. and U.S. Banks

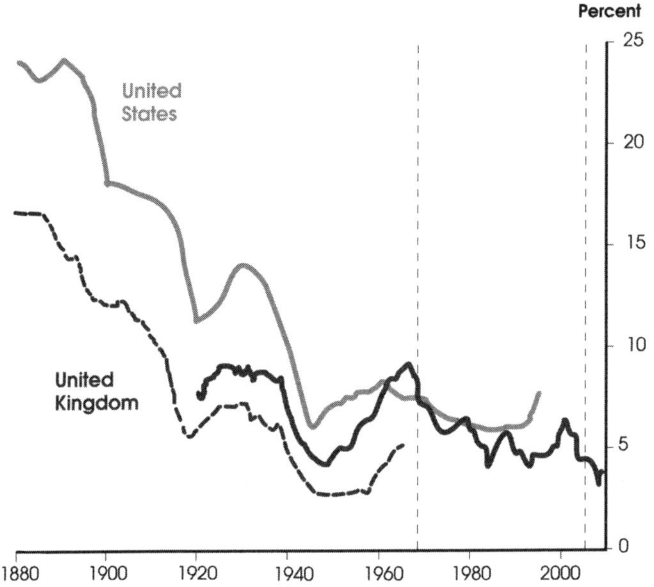

Source: Andrew Haldane, Bank of England, "The Contribution of the Financial Sector—Miracle or Mirage?," annex to speech given at the the Future of Finance Conference in London on July 14, 2010

growth in banking assets and loans, which exceeded GDP growth by a wide margin. In the U.S., banking assets relative to GDP increased fivefold over the past century; the increase was even more pronounced in the U.K., where banking assets relative to GDP increased by ten-fold. (See Figure 2-5). Most observers point to banking deregulation as the key driver of this process: in the absence of capital requirements, bank managers pursued increasingly leveraged growth strategies.

More interesting still is the combined effect of leverage and growth on bank profitability and risk. Other things being equal, doing banking intermediation with increasingly lower capital levels should increase return on equity (ROE) given that the cost of debt is substantially lower than cost of equity; but it should also introduce higher volatility on ROE. Figure 2-6 shows that this is unambiguously the case.

Prior to the great wave of financial deregulation of the 1960s, when banks had capital levels in the 10 to 15 percent range, or even

Figure 2-5. Size of the U.S. and U.K. Banking Systems Relative to GDP

U.S. Banking Assets As % of GDP   U.K. Banking Assets As % of GDP

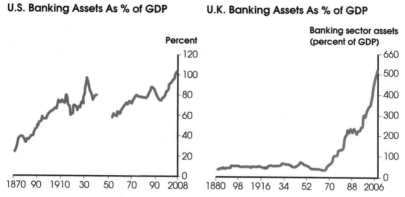

Source: Andrew Haldane, Bank of England, "The Contribution of the Financial Sector—Miracle or Mirage?," annex to speech given at the the Future of Finance Conference in London on July 14, 2010

Figure 2-6. Return on Equity (ROE) in the U.K. Financial Sector

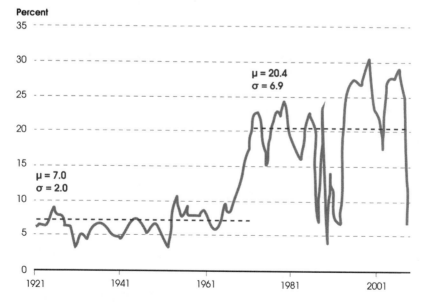

Source: Andrew Haldane, Bank of England, "The Contribution of the Financial Sector—Miracle or Mirage?," annex to speech given at the the Future of Finance Conference in London on July 14, 2010

higher, ROE was low (7 percent on average) but also extremely stable, with a standard deviation around 2 percent. In the last five decades, however, when banks lowered capital ratios to 5 percent or less, ROE soared on average to the 20 percent mark, and the standard deviation rose threefold. In other words, the trend toward lower capitalization levels became a very effective tool to boost ROE. It came at the expense of making equity much more risky and therefore, from the viewpoint of investors, subject to a higher cost of capital.

Investor perception of bank equity risk is best captured by the so-called beta coefficient, which measures the relative riskiness of bank stock prices compared with the overall market. Figure 2-7 shows banking-sector betas over the last two decades, estimated for a large sample of more than a hundred listed banks from all over the world. Historically, betas hovered around 1, but from 2004 onward the coefficient rose to 1.5 and above. In fact, the volatility of bank stocks has deviated from the trend for most other industries and has converged with the levels observed for commodities. Bank stocks have become extremely procyclical.

Banks may use the long-term trends on leverage, growth, and

Figure 2-7. Stock Betas for the World's 100 Largest Listed Banks (12-Month Moving Average)

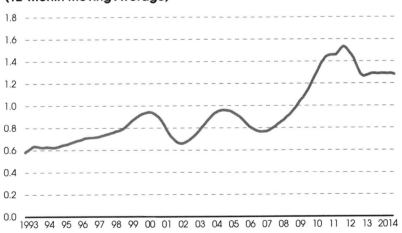

Source: Afi, Analistas Financieros Internacionales, S.A., estimates based on Bloomberg L.P.

profitability to assess the most likely consequences of increased capital requirements:

- Banking assets will grow at a much slower rate than in the past, and they might even decline if banks experience difficulties adjusting to the new capital requirements.
- As a consequence of the first point, there will be winners and losers. In the very long run, a significant increase in capital requirements—let's say twofold—should have a neutral effect. Banks will need more capital, but its cost will come down as investors become aware of the lower associated risk.
- The problem is how to get from today's low levels of capital to a new long-run steady state requiring much higher levels of capital. The transition will necessarily be easier for some banks than others, depending on their ability to generate internal funds and/or to persuade investors. Some banks will survive the journey while others will not.
- For those banks that survive, an acceptable ROE at endpoint— that is, when higher capital ratios translate into lower perceived risk for bank equity—could be in the range of 8 percent to 10 percent. This is clearly lower than in the precrisis period, but much higher than current ROE at most banks in crisis-hit mature markets, while most emerging markets, as well as some developed ones—in Australia, Canada, Scandinavia, and the U.S., for example—are ahead of this already. Given that profit forecasts are low for banks in most developed countries, the search for such a cruising level of ROE will have to rest on improvements in operating costs and revenue productivity, effectively moving to a new business model, as described in chapter 6.

NEW AND SIMPLER RISK MEASURES

Changes in the levels of required capital are not the only shifts that banks will need to pay attention to. The whole structure of capital requirements that has been in place during the last decades rested on the measurement of risk-weighted assets (RWAs). Basel I measured RWAs according to an extremely simple scale with 4 points, while Basel II incorporated a much wider scale based on ratings—both external and internal. This opened the road for a highly discretionary approach from banks on how to comply, as each followed its own internal models. Nowadays, the trend is toward much more complex risk measurement, which imposes time-consuming tasks and procedures on both banks and regulators.

The Bank of England's Haldane[3] documents that new regulatory requirements put in place over the last three decades have led to a twentyfold increase in the number of forms banks need to fill out, an increase in the number of employees devoted to compliance, and an even larger increase in staff at the regulatory agencies. And yet, such an inflated regulatory structure was unable to prevent risk losses and to differentiate between good and bad banks. Moreover, changes in regulation expanded the opportunities for arbitrage and made comparisons between banks, or even banking systems, more difficult.

A clear example of those arbitrage opportunities and lack of comparability lies in risk-weighted assets (RWA), the cornerstone of capital requirements under the Basel II regime, as capital requirements were established relative to RWA. Calculations based on a wide sample of international banks, however, demonstrate that there is no statistical association between RWA density (RWA over total assets) on the one hand, and stock volatility or credit ratings on the other.

In fact, determining RWA density is subject to a tremendous amount of subjectivity, especially in large banks using internally based models; it therefore offers little value when it comes to predicting distress. A recent study by Mike Mariathasan and Ouarda Merrouche[4] is sufficiently clear in this respect. It separates banks according to whether they have been resolved—bank resolution being equivalent to a failure without liquidation—or not, and within each sample it analyzes RWA density before and after banks were allowed to use the advanced approach to internally based ratings.

While banks that performed well (not resolved) had not previously exhibited a significant change in RWA density, banks that failed had been able to produce significantly lower RWA densities thanks to the use of advanced methods. This evidence shows that there has been considerable room for regulatory arbitrage, while rendering RWA of little value in terms of predicting bank distress.

The evidence indicating that existing regulations do not distinguish between good and bad banks is forcing regulators to rethink the benefits of complex risk-measurement models, and to reconsider the advantages of pure unweighted leverage ratios. As a matter of fact, some recent comparisons performed by the Bank of International Settlements (BIS) conclude that pure leverage ratios are a better predictor of bank stability (capacity to face adverse scenarios) than the complex solvency ratio based on RWA, which tends to be opaque and prone to manipulation. However, one should not expect regulators to abandon RWA calculations altogether, but to supplement them with requirements based on a pure unweighted leverage ratio, as a backstop and cross-check.

Adding a leverage ratio as a complement to RWA-based measures strengthens their validity and comprehensiveness as a risk measure. The argument for a framework that combines the two metrics is also supported by the fact that it is difficult to manipulate one without affecting the other, typically in the opposite direction. For example, an upward shift in portfolio risk might leave the leverage ratio unaffected, but it should increase risk-weighted assets. Conversely, investments in assets with underestimated risk, such as highly rated tranches of collateralized debt obligations prior to the crisis, would increase the denominator of a leverage ratio that incorporates derivatives exposures.

Additionally, it is likely that regulators will take steps to improve the reliability of internal risk measurement in banks through more stringent requirements for model approval. Tighter requirements can mitigate some of the variability that arises from statistical factors. An obvious example is a minimum length of time over which the model must be estimated, possibly conditioned on whether the sample covers a full credit cycle. More demanding standards of approval also strengthen the confidence of outsiders in model estimates.

Finally, new regulatory requirements will need to be supplemented by more market discipline through an improvement in outsiders' understanding of risk-weight calculations. Doing so requires greater transparency regarding the characteristics of internal models. Greater comparability of the disclosures that banks make about the structure and performance of their internal models will help analysts and outside stakeholders assess the relative strength of banks, and it should translate into more transparency and an enhanced ability to discriminate between banks.

All these new requirements regarding capital levels, and especially more reliable and transparent risk measurements models, will have deep and lasting implications for the management of banks' balance sheets. In the first place, banks will have to be much more selective in terms of allocation of capital to business lines, abandoning those where the capital needed is too high compared with the expected return. At the same time, banking products, especially the most capital-consuming ones, will have to adjust their pricing to the new capital requirements. Finally, excessive capital consumption in some products or business lines could act as an incentive to turn them into shadow banking, as we will analyze in chapter 3.

THE CONSEQUENCES OF SIZE AND COMPLEXITY

One of the most salient and controversial issues on the new regulatory agenda is how to deal with large and complex banks, both domestically and internationally. The issue has been raised as part of efforts to address systemic risk, and to reduce the increased moral hazard in large banks that benefit from the "too big to fail" principle.

Bank Size and Systemic Risk

The banking sector has grown in size and concentration over the last four decades. Financial liberalization, and particularly the repeal of the Glass-Steagall Act in 1999, started a "race to the bottom" between the U.S. and the U.K. in terms of lower regulatory standards to woo financial firms. The most important outcome of this process was increasing concentration, through a sustained reduction in the overall number of banks, as well as an increase in the market share of the largest.

While a higher concentration has clear benefits in terms of banking efficiency (see chapter 3), it generates acute problems from the point of view of financial stability if it produces increased expectations of state support for the banking system. These expectations translate into lower financing costs for the largest banks, and these lower costs in turn act as an incentive for further expansion and concentration, which in turn promotes the "too big to fail" dilemma. The implicit support for the largest banks has been widely documented by Haldane,[5] and has translated in the last decade into two to three notches of improvements in the credit ratings scale. Such an important implicit subsidy for large and complex banking groups carries the risk of generating an endless race for growth and concentration. Such a trend has important implications for competitive structure in banking systems, and market share of the largest five or ten banks has increased considerably in most developed countries during the past two decades.

From the point of view of prudential regulation, however, more worrying than those effects on market competition is the potential emergence of perverse incentives whereby large banks protected by such an implicit subsidy race to grow at the expense of incurring excessive risk levels, and therefore increase the chances that the contingent support from the state is needed.

To document the extent of such a "race to the top," we, the authors, estimated a measure of systemic risk (using stock market beta) for a large sample of international banks, grouped by size, and for two different periods: 2007, as representative of precrisis risk perception, and 2012, the most recent available year, which should take into consideration expectations of new, postcrisis regulations.

The results, as can be seen in Figure 2-8, are clear enough. Betas are today 30 percent higher than they were before the crisis for banks of all sizes. On the other hand, there is a positive relationship between bank size and systemic risk, with the largest banks (with assets greater than $1 trillion) displaying the largest betas. As long as diversification possibilities, which could help reduce risk, are larger for the biggest banks, we interpret their persistently higher betas as evidence that the largest banks are perceived as riskier due to enhanced moral hazards.

Bank growth beyond a certain size imposes severe contingent burdens on the government as the implicit guarantee threatens to become explicit. Not surprisingly, the regulatory agenda has been especially concerned with the systemic risk inherent in large and complex banking organizations. Specifically, two regulatory measures have been imposed to deal with the problem.

Figure 2-8. Betas for Different Bank Sizes

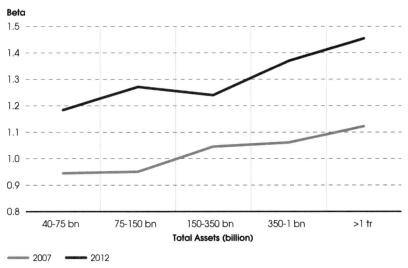

Note: Beta measures the sensitivity of stock prices to general market movements (as an example, beta 1.5 indicates that banks react by 50 percent bigger than market movements, either upward or downward.)

Source: Afi, Analistas Financieros Internacionales, S.A., based on stock market data for 100 large quoted banks worldwide

The first measure is a capital surcharge to be imposed on systemically important financial institutions (SIFIs). The Basel Committee on Banking Supervision has published a methodology for measuring the systemic relevance of banks on the basis of several parameters, including size, complexity of business, level of connectivity with the rest of the system, and so on. Five "buckets"—each representing a different degree of "systematicity"—were defined, with a capital surcharge ranging from 1 percent for the lowest to 3.5 percent for the highest. The Financial Stability Board, which serves to coordinate national financial authorities and international standard-setting bodies, endorsed those methodologies and published the list of banks in each bucket. Banks must come up with the additional capital by 2016.

The second set of regulatory measures proposed to deal with the "too big to fail" problem are of a more structural nature. The systemic surcharge has been widely considered to be a move in the right direction, one that eliminates, or at least partially compensates for, the implicit public subsidies and the associated perverse incentives created by this moral hazard. Critics point out, however, that strategic behavior on the part of banks could produce the opposite effect from that intended because a bank's presence on the list of systemically important institutions leads it to be perceived by the market as more likely to benefit from the implicit public subsidy, driving the cost of capital down and hence promoting further growth and expansion.

Structural Reforms: Separation of Activities

In an effort to discourage systemic banks from growing bigger, other types of regulatory measures of a more structural nature, have been advanced to deal with systemic risk. The most groundbreaking measures are those that impose a mandatory separation of commercial banks from banks dealing in securities and from investment banking in general. These measures impact large and complex banks in particular, as they are more prone to be bound by the mandatory separation of activities.

Proposals in that direction have been developed almost simultaneously in the U.S. (the Volcker Rule), the U.K. (the Vickers Commission), and the European Union (Liikanen Report[6]). Although there are differences in terms of the activities considered to be in one or the other category (see Table 2-3), these reform efforts have their rationale in common. The idea is to isolate basic financial intermediation, which is thought of as vital for the economy, from other, much riskier banking activities that do not deserve to benefit from the same implicit government guarantee. Regardless of where exactly the line is drawn and the vehicle used to separate activities, the proposals create a new landscape for financial services.

Table 2-3. A Stylized Comparison of Structural Reform Proposals in the U.S., E.U., and U.K.

	Volcker	Liikanen	Vickers
Broad approach	**Institutional separation** of commercial banking and certain invesment activities	**Subsidiarization:** proprietary and higher-risk trading activity have to be placed in a separate legal entity	**Ring fencing:** structural separation of activities via a ring fence for retail banks
Deposit-taking institution may:			
Deal as principal in securities and derivatives	No	No	No
Engage in market-making	Yes	No	No
Perform underwriting business	Yes[1]	Yes	Restricted
Hold non-trading exposures to other financial intermediaries	Unrestricted	Unrestricted	Restricted (inside the group)
Holding company with banking and trading subsidiaries	Not permitted	Permitted	Permitted
Geographical restrictions	No	No	Limitations for ring fenced banks in the U.K. to provide services outside the European Economic Area

[1]Underwriting in response to client/counterparty demand.

Source: Leonardo Gambacorta and Adrian van Rixtel, *Structural Bank Regulation Initiatives: Approaches and Implications*, BIS Working Papers, No 412, 2013

Basic intermediation between deposits and loans is expected, under the new regime, to be isolated from any losses incurred in riskier banking activities. Additionally, separation will prevent investment banking from flourishing, thanks to implicit or explicit state support, such as deposit guarantee schemes, liquidity supply by central banks, and other mechanisms that benefit commercial banks. Last, but not least, separation is also intended to encourage the reorganization and reshaping of the banking organizations that currently dominate the sector by reducing their complexity and probably their size, and therefore making them easier to manage, more transparent, and simpler to resolve in cases of stress.

On January 29, 2014, the European Commission published a set of proposals, along the lines of the aforementioned Liikanen Report, signaling a structural reform in the E.U. banking sector. Specifically, it imposes severe limitations on the trading activities that can be performed by the largest banks.

Banks bound by the new limitations are those considered the largest and most complex E.U. banks with significant trading activities. The yardstick for inclusion is two-pronged: (1) total assets in excess of 30 billion euros, and (2) trading activities amounting to more than 70 billion euros, or 10 percent of total assets. Some thirty banks across Europe are expected to rise above those levels, and therefore will be subject to the proposed limitations, which are basically of a dual nature:

1. A full prohibition to perform proprietary trading in financial instruments and commodities, that is, trading on its own account for the sole purpose of making profit for the bank, as this activity is perceived to entail many risks but no tangible benefits for the bank's clients or the wider economy.

2. Other risky trading activities (such as market-making, complex derivatives, and securitization operations) should be transferred to separate legal trading entities within the group ("subsidiarization"). This aims to avoid the risk that banks would get around the

ban on the prohibition of certain trading activities by engaging in hidden proprietary trading that becomes too significant or highly leveraged and can potentially put the whole bank and wider financial system at risk. Banks will have the option of not separating activities if they can show to the satisfaction of their supervisor that the risks generated are mitigated by other means.

The new limitations in banking will be binding in two phases: the prohibition will start at the beginning of 2017, while the transfer of activities will take place no later than July 1, 2018. According to Michel Barnier, Commissioner for Internal Market and Services, "Today's proposals are the final cogs in the wheel to complete the regulatory overhaul of the European banking system."

These new regulations bring about novel challenges, especially for large, universal banks with an international presence:

- Banks will need to adapt their overall strategy and organizational structure, and rethink their business lines, including abandoning some of them.
- Allocation of capital between business lines will also be made more complex, as restrictions will be imposed on the amount of capital required by each of them, with an explicit prohibition to cross-subsidize losses between activities on each side of the separating line.
- These challenges will be more demanding for banks operating in different national jurisdictions, so long as the separating lines are dissimilar in each of them, making it more difficult for them to optimize global capital allocation and strategies.
- Banks will also need to pay particular attention to the needs of more complex customers—especially businesses and corporations—whose needs may cross the boundaries of ring fences (where a portion of a bank's assets have been deliberately separated financially to provide greater protection) across jurisdictions.

CONSUMER PROTECTION

As extensive as new regulatory requirements concerning capital adequacy are, other areas of regulation will likewise transform the financial services landscape. Issues relating to consumer protection are a high priority in the new regulatory agenda; these new regulations are intended to help restore public confidence in banking, which has been severely damaged by the crisis.

There have been numerous cases of detrimental behavior and inappropriate conduct of various types, including mis-selling of products, failing to properly rate benchmark-setting processes, and evading taxation or laundering money. These and other undesirable business practices (not to mention the huge amount of public money needed to save banks from decisions made by well-paid executives) have raised wide public attention, as well as placing under suspicion the fiduciary duty of treating clients' money with the same care as you would treat your own. The attempt to separate intermediation activities from riskier investment activities manifests itself in terms of consumer protection. This new wave of regulation is in response to the dodgy and dangerous practices of many banks in Europe and the U.S., which put bank profits ahead of customer interests. The separation of activities is an attempt to enshrine the basic principle that banking at the retail level should be designed to serve the everyday financial needs of most of us: safekeeping deposits, saving, small loans, mortgages, credit, and insurance. The separation principle attempts to isolate those basic functions from other, riskier ones.

The importance given to consumer protection issues in the new regulatory agenda manifests itself in the regulatory architecture that is being adopted in most developed countries. Far from an old-fashioned approach that specialized regulators according to the nature of the business performed by financial services firms— banking, insurance, or capital markets—the new approach tends to favor the so-called "twin peaks" model. Under this new regime, two regulatory bodies with similar authority would coexist: one dedicated to assuring the financial stability and solvency of markets and intermediaries, and the other dedicated to guaranteeing that the practices and conduct of banks are aligned with their customers' rights and that the banks operate in their customers' interests. The establishment of the Consumer Financial Protection Bureau in the U.S. in 2011 and the recent separation of the former Financial Services Authority into two entities (Prudential Regulation Authority and Financial Conduct Authority) in the U.K., with the aforementioned goals in mind, is a first step in that direction, and sooner or later it will be followed by other regulatory bodies worldwide.

Regardless of the specific format in terms of regulatory bodies, there are several consumer protection requirements or rules of conduct that will be imposed on banks to guarantee that they treat customers fairly, and therefore fulfill their fiduciary duty. The main areas of concern regarding consumer protection are:

- **Financial literacy and education, or rather the lack of it.** This is an extremely important issue, especially given the increasing complexity and diversity of some financial products; a lack of understanding of financial products may result in consumers not being aware of the risks they assume or of the consequences of their contracting with the bank.

- **Mis-selling of complex saving products.** This raises an issue related to the aforementioned point on financial literacy, but also to alleged misconduct by bank employees in carrying out their relationship with customers. Steps are being taken by regulators to include additional transparency rules or some type of "labeling" of financial products according to their complexity and/or risk.

- **Managing conduct, staff culture, and incentives.** Regulators want to make sure that banks develop internal standards of conduct and appropriate incentives across all levels of organization, to ensure that all employees have customer service and satisfaction at the top of their scale of priorities.

- **Indebtedness and responsible credit.** Given the severe consequences for consumers arising from over-indebtedness (foreclosures, arrears, etc.), this topic is attracting increasing attention from regulators. Many countries have already taken steps to address this issue, including regulating the conditions under which a mortgage can be granted (maximum debt to income or to wealth, etc.) and developing codes of conduct that lenders must follow.

- **Bank account fees and charges.** Consumers' complaints about excessive charges, lack of transparency, and accuracy about pricing are quite extensive. They often lead to customer refunds, either at the behest of a supervisory authority or through the bank's own decision. Regulation will get more exigent in this area, with more stringent requirements in terms of transparency or even caps on fees charged for some services. As a step forward in these transparency requirements, it is not hard to imagine a future where regulators publish regular data on customer satisfaction with each individual bank.

- **Technology and security.** While it is an essential component in the new banking model, the fast speed of technological developments associated with the retail payments market raises security concerns. This is of special concern for the new banking channels such as Internet and mobile payments, as these technological developments have often been accompanied by increasingly sophisticated methods of fraud. This is why security and confidentiality concerns will be a permanent issue on the regulators' agenda.

- **Indices/benchmark manipulations.** The scandals surrounding the manipulation, or the lack of representativeness, of some of the most widely used financial indices (Libor, Euribor, and some foreign exchange crossings) have triggered a fresh wave of public revulsion about bankers' attitudes toward customers. Regulatory authorities have reacted by imposing severe penalties for banks with proven misconduct in these areas. They have also provided new rules and principles for the governance of those indices.

These are just some examples—certainly the most important ones—that highlight the importance of customer protection in the new regulatory agenda. Customer protection, however, is not only an issue of specific regulations but also of banks' legitimacy if they are to recover customer confidence and trust. We devote chapter 4 entirely to legitimacy issues.

NEW TAXES

The enormous amount of public money that many countries had to spend to rescue the banking system has generated a tidal wave of opinion about introducing new taxes on banks, in order to recover some of the public money spent. As early as September 2009, the G20 summit empowered the IMF to "prepare a report as to how the financial sector could make a fair and substantial contribution toward paying any burden associated with government intervention to repair the banking sector." New forms of taxes on different aspects of banking activity and/or profitability are clearly to be expected as part of the new regulatory agenda.

Taxes in general serve two different purposes: to add to government revenues and to influence an economic agent's behavior. This dichotomy is especially important when applied to banking business. The banking crisis has imposed severe burdens on governments everywhere. It has increased public debt as a consequence of the massive rescue packages tendered, and it has created negative externalities caused by a deteriorated banking system unable to perform its basic function of providing credit. Seen in this context, new bank taxes might be viewed as a way of recovering the cost of public support of the banking system, or even as a way of creating a reserve fund to ensure that taxpayers' money will not be used for bank bailouts in the future.

Alternatively, looking at the second function performed by taxes, new bank taxes might be used as part of the prudential regulations aimed at discouraging banks from taking excessive risks. Some even point out that taxes are a way of curbing the growth of the finance industry (IMF 2010, EC 2010), thought to have grown far beyond a point where marginal contribution to economic growth becomes negative, as we will analyze in chapter 3.

Regardless of which of those justifications is invoked to impose new taxes on banks, regulators and policy makers should ask themselves whether new taxation on banks will be effective, especially given a global context in which banks are able to move activities across jurisdictions. In such cases, only internationally coordinated approaches to new taxes will be effective. Recent studies show that effective tax rates on banks from OECD countries have come down consistently during the last three decades and, most importantly, the effective tax rate has consistently been much smaller than the statutory tax rates.[7] We observe a similar trend, using OECD data, in Figure 2-9. Banks have been able to find ways of consistently reducing their tax bill below the statutory tax rates, raising some doubts about the effectiveness of new bank taxes.

Additional consideration has to be given to the ability of banks to pass through taxes to customers, by way of increasing the rates charged to loans or by reducing the rates paid on deposits. This is most likely to occur when banks enjoy market power; for this reason, any new bank tax should be viewed only in the context of measures that seek to address an increase in the competitiveness of the banking system.

The debate on the effectiveness of new bank taxes, and especially

Figure 2-9. Bank Implicit Tax Rates for the Main OECD Countries

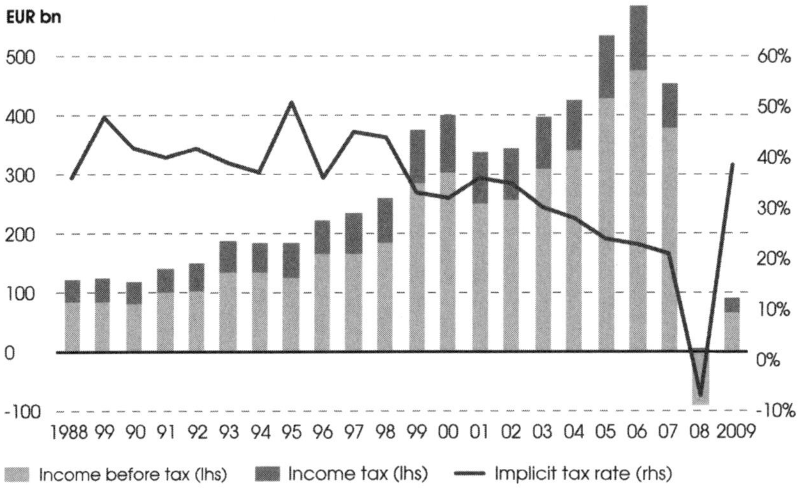

EUR bn

Income before tax (lhs)   Income tax (lhs)   —— Implicit tax rate (rhs)

Source: Afi, Analistas Financieros Internacionales, S.A., based on OECD Data

the need for further international coordination, is especially important in light of the European Union's proposal to establish a new financial transaction tax (FTT). It will impose an E.U.-wide tax rate of 0.1 percent for all equity and bond transactions, and 0.01 percent for derivative transactions between financial firms. The E.U. proposal is an attempt to harmonize, across several European countries, different financial activities and their respective taxes.

In order to facilitate identification and collection from the transactions involved, the E.U. proposal rests on the residence principle of taxation regardless of the counterparty's location. However, a recent pronouncement by E.U. Legal Council points out some legal problems regarding the interpretation of the residence principle, as it distorts competition and impacts fiscal competencies of member states outside the FTT area (like the U.K.). If, as expected following such a pronouncement, the residence principle is dropped, FTT will lose effectiveness on derivatives activities and remain effective only for securities (debt and equity) issued by entities in the FTT area.

A widespread criticism has arisen about this approach, as it may generate adverse extraterritorial effects for non-participating jurisdictions, or even influence the location of financial activity. Strong doubts are also in place regarding the true effectiveness of such a tax. It is unlikely that trading volumes will remain undamaged by the new tax, therefore lowering the base on which the tax will be applied. Additionally, it is unrealistic to assume that FTT is a cost only to banks, and that they will not pass the costs on to end users.

Toward a European Banking Union

The biggest victim of the 2008 crisis eventually became the Eurozone, where dubious risk-management practices interacted with the sovereign debt problem within the constraints of a monetary union, to create one of the most intractable financial debacles in history. Before the crisis, banks in the Eurozone displayed a differential behavior when it came to taking on new risks, especially those related to government securities and the real estate sector. Liquidity flowed to the most aggressive banks. After the crisis started, the failure of the usual financial channels to provide enough liquidity led to a systemic crisis that has left many financial institutions in a very dire situation.

The banking crisis proved to be most virulent in countries that had seen loan activity increase at rates higher than 20 percent, especially true in Ireland and Spain. By the end of 2008, outstanding bank loans as a percentage of GDP were 130 percent in Ireland and 145 percent in Spain, compared with 90 percent in Germany and 98 percent in France. Most of the loan growth in Ireland and Spain went to feed a housing and real estate bubble. In the wake of the bubble's bursting, banks throughout Europe required direct capitalization or other forms of government guarantees. The markets quickly started to discount the probability that they might end up translating private debt into public debt.

Contamination from bank support to public debt was, however,

Figure 2-10. Credit Default Swap Spreads for a Basket of European Countries and Banks (Basis Points, Weighted by Gross Debt)

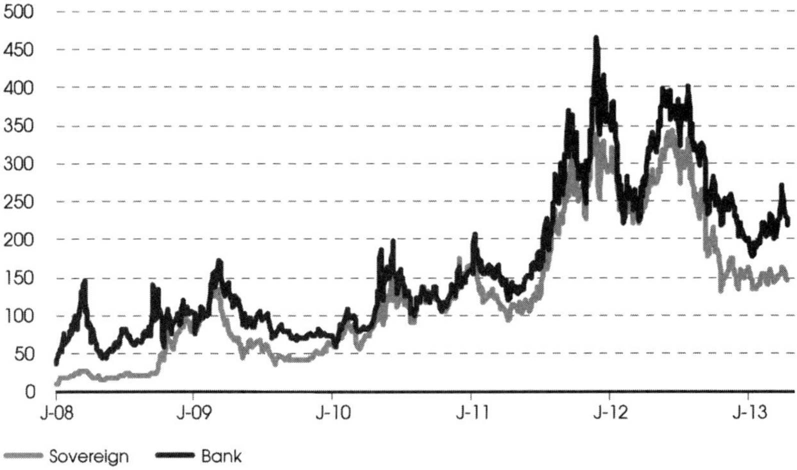

Source: Afi, Analistas Financieros Internacionales, S.A., based on Bloomberg L.P.

only the first step in a rapidly evolving vicious circle between banks and governments. Rising unemployment and declining tax revenue increased the financing needs of governments, and most of the new sovereign debt and the rollovers were placed with banks. In the absence of a truly credible monetary shock absorber, that vicious circle threatened to perpetuate itself. The evolution of credit default swaps (CDS) on a synthetic basket of European countries and banks, weighted by gross debt, displayed an increasing correlation (about 85 percent) and an upward trend until the summer of 2012. That was when the European Central Bank (ECB) announced its new Outright Monetary Transactions (OMT) program of direct sovereign bond purchases (see Figure 2-10).

The most clear and direct consequence of such an alignment between banks and sovereign risks (Treasury bonds) is that funding possibilities for European banks in the wholesale market became tied to the situation in the market for sovereign debt. Given that the rating agencies usually consider that bank ratings, from any given

Figure 2-11. Relationship Between Bank and Sovereign Ratings (2013)

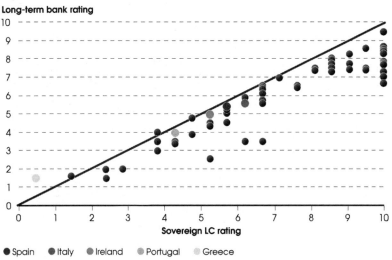

Source: Afi, Analistas Financieros Internacionales, S.A., estimation based on credit ratings

country (see Figure 2-11), are limited by their respective sovereign ratings, European banks' ability to access wholesale markets became severely limited.

The increasing correlation between the fortunes of banks and governments led to a situation in which two banks with the same solvency and profitability ratios, one headquartered in Spain and the other in Germany, would be able to borrow at dramatically different rates. Under such conditions, the interbank market in the Eurozone could not function properly.

This increasing fragmentation of European banking markets, in spite of monetary union, also manifested itself at the level of retail deposits, which lie at the core of the European banking system. As Figure 2-12 shows, retail deposits were more expensive—by at least 100 basis points—in the weakest economies than in the strongest ones. If we add the fact that deposits moved from weaker to stronger economies' banks, the result was a complete fragmentation across the different banking systems in the Eurozone, with extremely adverse

Figure 2-12. Average Yields on Retail Banking Deposits

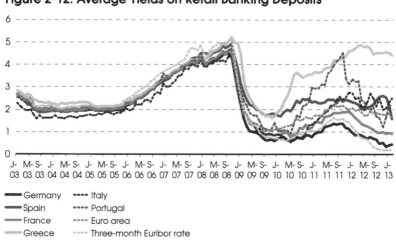

Source: Afi, Analistas Financieros Internacionales, S.A., based on ECB data

consequences for households' and companies' finances. Two similar companies, one located in a weak country and another in a stronger one, face different financing costs—up to 3 percent or 4 percent differential—and therefore the competitive position of companies operating in weak countries is severely damaged.

It follows from here that the Eurozone would not be sustainable without a full and credible banking union, in order to break the vicious circle between banks and sovereign risk, and to overcome the financial fragmentation affecting competitiveness of nonfinancial companies, especially small and medium enterprises (SMEs).

Important steps have been taken during the last year and a half toward establishing a banking union whose end point will not arrive until ten years' time, but whose main constituents have already been established, signaling a no-return move toward a full banking union.

A truly credible banking union rests on two basic pillars: a single supervisory mechanism and a single resolution mechanism. The first one is a precondition for homogeneous trust in European banks, regardless of their country of origin. The second one guarantees that depositors—and creditors in general—are treated similarly in case of bank failures, regardless of the home country of each bank. Both pillars have been approved by the European Parliament and are in the process of becoming fully operational.

The single supervisory mechanism (SSM) was approved by the European Parliament in September 2013, and will be fully operational by late 2014. It confers on the European Central Bank (ECB) direct supervisory powers over the largest banks in the euro area (some 130 banks, each with assets in excess of 30 billion euros, or 20 percent of their home country's GDP), and gives the ECB monitoring responsibility for the national authorities that supervise smaller banks.

Prior to the ECB accepting supervision of the largest and most systemic European banks, a comprehensive exercise is being carried out in order to assess the health of those banks and ensure that they will enter the new supervisory regime under homogeneous conditions and with no legacy assets. The comprehensive exercise is carried out jointly by the ECB and the European Banking Authority (EBA), and comprises three phases: a general risk assessment, an asset quality review, and a forward-looking (over a three-year horizon) stress test. The comprehensive exercise is expected to be completed by November 2014, before the ECB is due to assume its duties as common supervisor, and that exercise will signal which banks need some type of capital injection before being admitted to the new supervisory regime.

The parameters and methodologies used in the exercise, and especially in the stress test, are crucial for the credibility of the ECB as a future supervisor. Markets are expecting—or rather demanding—that the ECB conduct harsher stress test exercises than those performed in the past (mostly by the EBA, whose credibility ended up somewhat weakened).

The SRM was approved by the European Parliament in April 2014, in the context of a new directive on bank resolution. Under the new regime, private sector involvement (that of shareholders, bondholders, and large depositors) will be required in cases of bank failures. A minimum 8 percent of total liabilities will have to be bailed-in by those liability holders before any public money is invested in a bank subject to resolution.

Advances have also been made in the decision-making process about bank resolution, as well as on the size of the resolution fund to be created at the European level to serve as an effective and credible backstop. Regarding the first issue, the objective is to have as little bureaucracy as possible when a bank resolution is discussed, as speedy decisions are key in those cases. Regarding the second issue, the objective is to gradually move from country-specific resolution funds to a European-wide fund, in order to break the vicious circle between banks' troubles and their treasuries' ability to cope with them. A compromise solution has been reached on an eight-year transition period, during which time national funds will be progressively substituted by a pan-European fund, expected to reach 1 percent of total deposit in the euro area.

Since these transitional aspects have finally been approved, a true European banking union has started, whereby all banks will be subject to the same regulation and supervision, and their liability holders subject to the same burden-sharing rules. In such an environment, it is clear that banks' competitive strategies will need to be designed on a European-wide scope, regardless of the actual penetration of banks across different European countries.

CONCLUSION

Aware that former regulation was not able to prevent the deepest banking crisis in almost a century, authorities are imposing a complete overhaul of banking regulation. The new regulatory environment is being defined in order to avoid some of the perverse incentives that are thought to lie behind excessive risk taking by banks, as well as the asymmetric distribution of profits and losses in an industry that enjoys implicit benefits not available to other business sectors. From the point of view of banks themselves, while regulation acts as a restriction on some managerial degrees of freedom, it should not be seen as a hindrance. It may well create opportunities for banks to differentiate and to rebuild their reputations, as well as the reputation of the sector as a whole.

The main areas to be affected by the new regulatory changes, and potential effects on banks' management, are the following:

• Banks will be required to have much more capital, especially "core equity," as this crisis has demonstrated that the level of capital previously required was clearly insufficient to cover losses in adverse scenarios. Capital will be evaluated in terms other than solely risk-weighted assets, as these have proved to be highly subjective and not good predictors of bank difficulties. As a complement to risk-weighted capital, requirements will be made in terms of total assets (unweighted leverage ratio). This will have deep implications on banks' business models. Capital allocation to different business lines will have to be much more strict, and subsidies among lines will no longer be possible. Scarce capital will be allocated to those business lines able to generate appropriate return on equity, while many traditional lines will appear to be unprofitable, and will be abandoned.

• A better capitalized banking model should be seen by markets and investors as a less risky business model than that used in the past, and therefore required risk premia and return on equity should be lower, at least on a new steady state approach. At the end point, with capital ratios about 50 percent higher than in the past decades, required return on equity should stabilize around levels in the 8 percent to 10 percent range.

• The transition period, where banks are required to increase capital while markets have not yet assumed the new low-risk environment, opens clear opportunities for better-managed banks to rebuild their capital base sooner and at better conditions. As long as stock market valuations are substantially better for banks that exhibit better management performance, they will be able to issue shares and strengthen their capital base.

• Large and complex banks will be required to meet capital surcharges to cover the extra systemic risk they represent. This measure tries to counteract the so-called "too big to fail" advantage that large banks enjoy in terms of cheaper financing costs. In terms of banks managing their equity and return expectations, however, these additional requirements should not be seen as penalizing large banks because higher capital ratios are expected to translate into lower required return on equity.

• More importantly, large and complex banks will be forced to separate commercial banking activities (protected by government guarantees) from other, riskier banking activities on the investment side. These structural reforms aim at ring fencing core from noncore banking activities, and avoid the latter being subsidized by the former. Banks will have to adapt their organizational structure to these new separation principles, with challenges being posed for global banks present in different jurisdictions. As long as the ring-fence lines are not homogeneous across jurisdictions, global banks will have to manage their operational and organizational implications across the different geographical areas in which they operate.

• Consumer protection concerns will be at the core of the new regulatory landscape as a response to some alleged abuses by banks during the crisis, including mis-selling of financial products, indices manipulation, and excessive charges in payment operations. These, as well as security and confidentiality concerns—especially with the growth of mobile and Internet banking—will produce a regulatory agenda more friendly to customers. In this area, more than in any other, there are clear opportunities for banks to move proactively, even faster than regulation requirements, and differentiate from competitors. Banks should respond to these new consumer concerns not only by meeting the new regulatory standards, but by taking the lead in organization-wide cultural changes and incorporating strict codes of conduct that place customers' needs at the top of all employees' priorities.

- All of these regulatory changes brought about as a response to the crisis are going to alter the banking business significantly, with important implications that all banks will have to cope with. These range from a wholesale reappraisal of strategic purpose, not just to comply with regulations but to demonstrate commitment with a new view of socially useful banking. Cultural changes will need to be introduced in the same direction, and this implies aligning governance, incentives, and codes of conduct toward a new and clearly defined customer centricity. New requirements on capital and risk measures incorporate additional demands on risk governance, but also open the door for a more differentiated approach, as well as more intelligent and proactive data management.

- In addition to those regulatory changes affecting banking worldwide, banking in Europe is going to face the most sweeping structural reform ever seen, with the creation of a European Banking Union. A common regulatory and supervisory structure, combined with a common set of rights and risks for liability holders across European countries, creates a completely new competitive landscape in European banking. Regardless of the specialization of each bank across different business lines or geographical presence—with a heavy bias toward the country of origin—the new landscape will require all banks to be competitive on a European-wide basis.

CHAPTER 3

Competition

How much competition is desirable in banking, and to what extent banking competition has been affected by the crisis, are questions more open than ever. While nobody doubts that competition is good for customers in most sectors of the economy, the answer is much more complex and controversial in banking. Back in the summer of 2011, *The Economist*[1] hosted a vivid debate on the issue of competition in banking and its effects on financial stability. Well known for its liberal approaches to virtually all sectors of the economy, the magazine ended up supporting the notion that "more competition makes banking more dangerous."

The crisis is going to significantly alter the competitive structure of banking. This change may arise from the crisis itself or from different governmental responses to the crisis. Hundreds of banks have disappeared in developed countries, either liquidated or merged into stronger players, leading to an increasingly concentrated market. In some cases governments took majority stakes in failed institutions, with important implications for market structure and competition.

Regulatory pressures to separate core and noncore activities as well as market forces—stock market pressure in particular—will force banks to divest from business lines that are unprofitable or consume too much capital, focusing instead on activities in which they possess a competitive advantage. This process will create a new paradigm about size in banking. Size by itself is unlikely to be valued by markets, and certainly much less than profitability or financial strength. Within core activities, however, there will be room for economies of scale, both in basic bank operations and in data mining and business intelligence. Finally, the banking industry is also going to be transformed by the arrival of new players, either new banks or nonbank financial intermediaries.

China is perhaps the market in which this trend toward nonbank intermediation is growing the fastest, generating hopes for higher bank competition but also worries about potential sources of financial instability, especially given the impressive size that shadow and unregulated banking has attained in the country. It is in the context of these worries that new efforts are being made among international regulators to establish clear rules and more transparency on shadow banking activities.

These unstoppable trends open up challenges and opportunities for banks to adapt to a completely new competitive landscape, with several implications in terms of the basic attributes that make a bank competitive. One of them is the role played by technology, with a smaller reliance on relationship banking (soft information) and more emphasis on behavioral models. Although this method lends itself more to economies of scale, it is also replicable by other potential competitors inside or outside the banking industry.

Another important implication of the new competitive landscape has to do with the war to attract and retain talented professionals. Banks will find themselves competing with other sectors of the economy for the best people, at the same time that new regulations will impose severe restrictions on remuneration in banking as a way to break the perverse connection between payment systems and excessive risk taking.

FINANCIAL SYSTEMS:
BANKING VERSUS MARKET ORIENTED

Bank intermediation is only one of the two basic ways that finance flows in the economy; the other one is directly through capital markets. A simple starting point for comparing financial systems is to look at them in terms of their structural configuration, particularly whether they are based on bank-intermediated funding or market-channeled finance. In a bank-based system, banks are the crucial players in bringing funds from investors to nonfinancial corporations. They pool the resources of dispersed capital providers and play an important role as delegated monitors of the firms they lend to, on behalf of deposit holders.[2] In the market-based paradigm, it is predominantly through markets that firms interact with investors providing the capital. Here firms can more easily find funding by participating in markets for tradable securities, such as stocks or corporate bonds.

Traditionally, in Japan and continental Europe the role of banks has been much greater than in the United States, where markets play a larger role in transactions between providers and users of capital. Figure 3-1 clearly illustrates this structural difference among the world's largest financial systems in terms of the relative weight of banking intermediation versus direct market finance. Bank assets in Japan or the Eurozone are about the same order of magnitude as total debt securities outstanding, and three or four times as big as stock market capitalization. The dominance of banking assets over securities is even bigger in the Asia ex-Japan region. On the contrary, however, U.S. bank assets are significantly smaller (by about one-third) than total outstanding securities, considering both debt and stock markets.

An interesting question is whether financial systems' specialization toward banking or markets is changing over time, and to what extent the crisis might be pushing in one direction or the other. A

Figure 3-1. Bank Assets Compared to Equity and Debt Markets

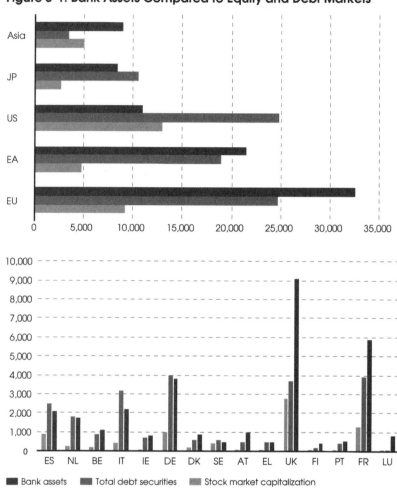

Source: *European Commission's High-Level Expert Group on Reforming the Structure of the E.U. Banking Sector*, chaired by Erkki Liikanen, Final Report, Brussels, October 2, 2012

school of thought closer to financial theorists, and especially those most aligned with efficient market postulates, would tend to support that as countries get more financially developed they tend to be more market oriented and less banking oriented. Some recent evidence produced by the Bank for International Settlements tends to support such an argument, although the evidence is far from conclusive: the share of bank credit in total credit decreases with financial development, as proxied by the total credit-to-GDP ratio, though this link is far from strong.

In fact, key disparities among countries in terms of the nature of their financial systems have somewhat subsided in the aftermath of the recent crisis, as the financial sector in many medium- and low-income countries was relatively isolated from the global turmoil, and therefore less affected by global liquidity shocks since 2008. In addition, financial institutions on average rebounded faster than markets, showing improvements in depth and efficiency after the crisis.

Turning to the banking share in the financial system, the variable that best reflects the level of activity is private credit, defined as credit to the private sector from deposit banks, expressed as a percentage of GDP, a measure also known as banking depth. Financial theory would predict that banking depth across different countries must be related to the level of development or per capita income. This is in fact what can be inferred from Table 3-1, which summarizes average and median bank depth (private credit to GDP) for countries grouped according to level of development as well as income level. On average, private credit clearly exceeds 100 percent of GDP in developed economies, while it represents only around 30 percent in developing economies and around 10 percent in lower-income countries.

Overall banking credit, however, can be a misleading indicator of banking activity, at least of profitable banking activity, as it can suffer from concentration with a few large customers. An alternative and more forward-looking view of banking activity is to examine the use of banking services by the largest segments of the population. A proxy for that metric is the number of banking relationships (accounts) per adult in the population. Table 3-2 shows the average and median values for that metric across different countries. The comparison clearly indicates again a large degree of heterogeneity between developed and emerging countries. While developed markets average more than 2,000 bank accounts per 1,000 adult people, developing markets average 500 or fewer.

Table 3-1. Private Credit to GDP (%)

Private credit to GDP (%)	Number of countries	Average	Median	Standard deviation	Min- imum	Max- imum	Weighted average*
World	173	56.3	38.8	54.6	3.2	361.7	89.9
By developed/ developing economies							
Developed economies	48	113.3	100.1	68.6	3.3	361.7	103.0
Developing economies	125	34.5	26.3	24.9	3.2	112.0	60.5
By income level							
High income	48	113.3	100.1	68.6	3.3	361.7	103.0
Upper middle income	49	48.6	44.5	28.0	8.0	112.0	67.8
Lower middle income	49	30.8	27.0	18.7	3.2	96.8	36.6
Low income	27	15.4	12.8	9.8	3.3	44.7	24.9
By region							
High income: OECD	30	124.0	109.4	52.2	43.2	228.2	103.7
High income: non-OECD	17	97.3	65.6	90.7	3.3	361.7	80.7
East Asia & Pacific	17	46.8	38.8	34.6	3.3	111.1	100.1
Europe & Central Asia	19	44.9	41.1	19.6	16.0	88.1	40.4
Latin America & Caribbean	29	41.5	32.0	24.2	12.3	112.0	33.4
Middle East & North Africa	12	34.5	29.1	26.0	5.5	71.8	32.1
South Asia	8	35.3	34.6	17.3	7.9	66.1	41.1
Sub-Saharan Africa	41	20.1	16.4	16.9	3.2	80.8	38.7

*Weighted average by current GDP. Note: OECD = Organisation for Economic Co-operation and Development.
Source: The World Bank, "Rethinking the Role of the State in Finance," *Global Financial Development Report 2013*

Two forward-looking implications can be drawn from these numbers. First, developing countries have clear growth potential, as less than half of their adult population is currently using banking services in their most basic form—a bank account. Second, developed countries, at the other extreme, probably are overbanked in terms of bank accounts per adult. As switching between banks becomes easier and faster, there is probably room to lower the average number of bank accounts held by the adult population in order to optimize bank-customer relationships.

A mirror image of such a difference in bank depth and penetration between developed and emerging countries is related to the different level of competition in each category. There are many different ways of measuring competition, but all of them will have a direct

Table 3-2. Bank Accounts at Commercial Banks (Per 1,000 Adults)

Accounts per thousand adults from commercial banks	Number of countries	Average	Median	Standard deviation	Min-imum	Max-imum	Weighted average*
World	79	904.7	584.2	1,147.3	2.4	7,185.2	1,339.0
By developed/ developing economies							
Developed economies	18	2,004.3	1,311.2	1,766.1	121.8	7,185.2	3,761.8
Developing economies	61	580.2	395.8	598.2	2.4	3,176.4	691.5
By income level							
High income	18	2,004.3	1,311.2	1,766.1	121.8	7,185.2	3,761.8
Upper middle income	21	921.1	902.7	534.1	38.0	2,015.2	997.9
Lower middle income	24	570.1	437.3	664.1	16.1	3,176.4	725.9
Low income	16	147.9	128.9	112.0	2.4	365.5	222.5
By region							
High income: OECD	12	2,320.2	1,581.8	1,945.7	513.6	7,185.2	3,933.9
High income: non-OECD	6	1,372.5	878.1	1,248.0	121.8	3,561.8	1,082.9
East Asia & Pacific	7	668.6	431.6	630.3	44.3	1,570.3	799.3
Europe & Central Asia	13	1,047.8	909.2	811.2	38.0	3,176.4	1,645.5
Latin America & Caribbean	7	873.6	667.2	587.6	329.4	2,015.2	967.0
Middle East & North Africa	7	385.9	343.3	295.6	77.4	873.0	384.7
South Asia	5	506.7	365.5	429.7	71.1	1,130.0	531.7
Sub-Saharan Africa	22	261.0	150.3	294.5	2.4	1,132.0	281.1

*Weighted average by total adult population. Note: OECD = Organisation for Economic Co-operation and Development.

Source: The World Bank, "Rethinking the Role of the State in Finance," *Global Financial Development Report 2013*

or indirect effect on the final measure of "value for customers," that is the lending-deposit spread, measuring the difference between the interest paid for deposits and the interest charged to credit.

Table 3-3 makes readily apparent the great difference between developed and emerging markets in terms of the lending-deposit spread. Developing countries display average spreads that are twice as large as those observed in developed countries, although the latter are also quite heterogeneous. The conclusion is clear-cut: developing and emerging markets are less saturated than developed ones, and allow for a much higher intermediation margin.

It would be wrong, however, to make a simple extrapolation and conclude that emerging countries will grow in banking assets, or

Table 3-3. Lending-Deposit Spread (%)

Lending-deposit spread (%)	Number of countries	Average	Median	Standard deviation	Min- imum	Max- imum	Weighted average*
World	129	7.7	6.3	6.4	0.1	41.5	6.9
By developed/ developing economies							
Developed economies	28	3.8	3.5	2.0	0.2	8.1	2.2
Developing economies	101	8.8	6.9	6.7	0.1	41.5	7.3
By income level							
High income	28	3.8	3.5	2.0	0.2	8.1	2.2
Upper middle income	43	6.7	6.2	5.3	0.1	34.0	6.5
Lower middle income	39	8.8	8.0	4.7	2.4	24.8	6.0
Low income	19	13.7	10.2	10.1	3.3	41.5	13.0
By region							
High income: OECD	14	2.6	2.7	1.2	0.2	4.7	1.9
High income: non-OECD	13	5.1	4.9	1.9	1.8	8.1	5.1
East Asia & Pacific	17	7.3	5.5	4.7	2.4	20.2	3.6
Europe & Central Asia	17	7.7	6.2	5.2	0.4	20.8	6.7
Latin America & Caribbean	27	9.6	7.2	6.8	4.1	34.0	16.9
Middle East & North Africa	10	4.6	4.9	2.6	0.1	9.5	4.6
South Asia	5	5.9	5.9	0.5	5.2	6.4	6.0
Sub-Saharan Africa	26	11.7	8.8	8.9	3.3	41.5	12.8

*Weighted average by total adult population. Note: OECD = Organisation for Economic Co-operation and Development.

Source: The World Bank, "Rethinking the Role of the State in Finance," *Global Financial Development Report 2013*

banking penetration, close to a level comparable to that in developed markets. The crisis of 2008 represents a stark reminder that excessive capacity and low margins invited banks to use leverage and other risky gimmicks to generate profits that a mature sector with high penetration could not deliver otherwise.

Research shows that there is indeed an optimal level of banking activity beyond which economic growth suffers. A recent study by Stephen Cecchetti and Enisse Kharroubi,[3] sponsored by the Bank for International Settlements and covering fifty countries (developed, emerging, and developing ones) over three decades, shows that bank depth follows an inverse U-shaped relationship with economic growth: increasing banking depth improves economic growth up to a point, after which it becomes detrimental. The turning point is estimated at a level somewhere around 90 percent of credit-to-GDP. When banking depth is measured by the share of bank employment as a percentage of the total, the turning point is estimated to be in the neighborhood of 3.8 percent.

Most developed countries, and especially those severely affected by the credit bubbles that preceded the current crisis (Spain, Ireland, the U.K., and the U.S. are among them), clearly exceed the optimal point. One may argue that they are overbanked in terms of outstanding bank credit or in terms of banking capacity.

Corrections have already started in most developed countries, although at a slow pace that will extend the process for more than an additional decade. Deleveraging will be especially intense in families and in nonfinancial firms, while it will be replaced by additional indebtedness by governments. But these, as well as the largest companies with investment opportunities to exploit, are sectors whose financial needs can be served outside the banking system.

EMERGING-MARKET BANKING

Excess banking capacity in developed countries stands sharply in contrast with the large growth potential of most emerging and developing countries. Dealing with this asymmetry represents a main challenge and opportunity for large banks adopting a global strategic approach. The most appropriate strategy across countries will be shaped by the balance between two opposing forces. On the one hand, regulatory burdens as well as government actions are likely to make ring fences proliferate, in turn making global strategies more difficult and pressing for additional levels of segmentation (ring fence). On the other hand, however, the expansive possibilities offered by mobile banking, and the ease with which it is possible to switch banks, will increase opportunities to exploit economies of scale and information across national jurisdictions.

These opportunities are especially suited for banking penetration in some emerging countries, where there is ample room for growth in banking services without incurring the fixed costs of establishing expensive branch networks. As the World Bank recognizes new technologies, particularly mobile banking and retail payment systems, are an essential pillar for financial inclusion and economic development, especially in less developed countries. One of the most cited examples in this regard is Kenya's M-Pesa™, today a leading provider of integral financial services in that country, and whose activity in mobile payment services started when the country was almost unbanked and had very low mobile phone penetration. This is the most clear example of innovation in mobile banking acting as a pull factor toward banking as well as other economic sectors. An opposite example could be found in Russia, which does extremely poorly in terms of mobile banking despite having one of the highest rates of mobile phone subscriptions in the world.

Regardless of the exceptions, advances in digital banking promise to be more dynamic in emerging countries than in high-income economies. Consumers who previously lacked banking access are quickly acquiring consumer technology, and therefore banks in those countries can create additional economic and social value by offering services such as easy-to-use savings products or information services to remote populations.

At the same time, mobile banking and payment technologies change the economic conditions of banking as they reduce the fixed cost of providing financial services. This reduction in fixed costs is especially relevant in countries with low population densities and low per capita income, precisely the environment that characterizes some of the most promising emerging countries.

By reducing their cost-to-serve, banks can capture new-to-bank customers more profitably without building inherent costs into the model. Strategies to achieve this include digital banking and extending distribution with partners. Several Latin American countries have witnessed an extensive use of correspondent banking networks. Mexico is probably the most significant exponent in this sense, with a banking network distribution in which traditional branches represent less than a quarter of total bank branches, versus almost two-thirds being correspondent branches, most of them located inside retail or convenience stores, like Walmart Inc., 7-Eleven Inc., or the OXXO Financial Services Inc., retail chain. Brazil and Colombia are other Latin American countries where correspondent banking is growing fast; regulators are helpful in this trend, as they allow greater flexibility in documentation and information requirements for small balance accounts.

Steps in this direction are critical to facilitate advances in banking penetration and financial inclusion in a faster and cheaper way than through traditional branches. Figure 3-2 displays the relationship between financial inclusion (measured by the percentage of adult population having an account with a formal bank) and traditional branch density (measured by branches per 100,000 adults) for a sample of emerging countries, using World Bank data for 2012. While a fitted regression line would point to a positive relationship between both variables (high branch density as a precondition for

Figure 3-2. Emerging Countries: Financial Inclusion Versus Branch Density

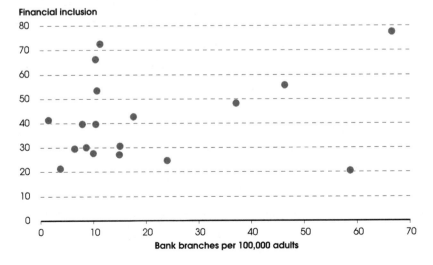

Source: World Bank

financial inclusion), the appearance of several countries close to the vertical axis points out some weakening of that relationship, thanks to distribution forms other than traditional bank branches.

When considering emerging countries' attractiveness for Western banks to expand into, however, care should be taken when selecting countries, as the crisis has shown that overexpansion without a justifiable business case can be a recipe for disaster. Banks should expand selectively, choosing geographies where they can leverage their domestic competitive advantages, and also where there are significant growth opportunities at reasonable risk levels.

To draw some lessons about which countries present better and more balanced growth opportunities, we have plotted in Figure 3-3 a sample of emerging countries in terms of banking saturation (measured by loans over GDP) and per capita income. The most attractive countries would be those in the lower-right quadrant (largest income and lowest saturation), Russia and Latin America being the most attractive according to those two parameters. At the other extreme (upper-left quadrant), there are countries with higher banking saturation and lower per capita income, China being the clearest exponent.

China's extreme position as the emerging country with the highest ratio of loans to GDP is the result of a long-lasting credit bubble that has taken place in that country, raising some concerns about the stability of a system that has multiplied its size by a factor of four in about a decade. Concerns are even higher when it is considered that almost one-third of the outstanding credit in the Chinese economy has been granted by lightly regulated shadow banking, discussed later in this chapter.

Such a huge growth of bank credit in the most populated country in the world has other important implications for the overall banking system structure, and that is the appearance of Chinese banks at the highest positions in the rankings of the world's largest and most profitable banks. While in 2005 the world's twenty-five largest banks by market capitalization were located in advanced countries, currently at

Figure 3-3. Emerging Countries: Loans to GDP Versus Per Capita GDP

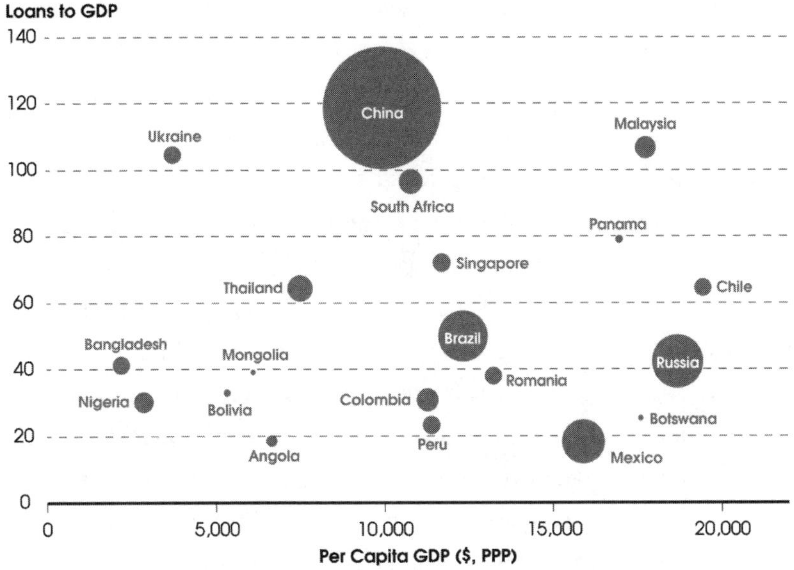

Loans to GDP

Source: World Bank

least eight are in emerging markets, and four of them are in China; in fact, the four largest Chinese banks are among the world's ten largest.

Recent turmoil in emerging market economies may slow down the enormous growth rate observed in the last decade, but it will probably not be sufficient to curb a clear trend toward an increasing role of emerging countries' banks in the league of major world banks, as they are bound to grow faster than their counterpart Western banks.

BANK COMPETITION, PROFITABILITY, AND EFFICIENCY

The recent financial crisis and some of the measures taken by governments, among them injecting vast amounts of money into problem banks or setting up expansionary monetary policies, may end up producing perverse effects on competitive structures. Exit strategies from those exceptional measures will be crucial for preventing those distortions from affecting competitive structures.

It is widely acknowledged that banking crisis management often requires governments to take ownership of banks or offer banks guarantees in order to maintain financial stability and banks' capacity to lend. They may even exercise some control over banks to orchestrate their restructuring. In such exceptional circumstances, competition policy should acknowledge the trade-off between the need for effective bank resolution and preserving a level playing field. Policy must strike a balance between the two. Competition policy might also be temporarily altered to allow for a higher banking system concentration when deemed necessary. An example in this direction was Lloyds TSB's acquisition of the failing HBOS plc, in the U.K. In normal times, the scale of the acquisition would have triggered actions by competition authorities; yet the U.K. government waived the operation from being reviewed by the competition commission. These types of exceptions on competition surveillance are made to allow banks to rebuild charter values or to facilitate the shrinking of a previously overexpanded banking system.

The temporary presence of the public sector creates important challenges and opportunities for the rest of the banks. In the short term, state presence may constitute an exit barrier that allows some inefficient banks to be kept alive, and this will generate unhealthy competition. This threat can be avoided by the imposition of severe restrictions on banks receiving public support, to prevent them from using competition distortion practices, such as paying higher interest on deposits or explicitly advertising that state presence gives them extra security over other banks. These types of restrictions have been especially noteworthy in the European Union, where the European Commission has invoked state aid rules to impose severe restrictions, or even sanctions, on bailed-out banks across Europe, with cases including big names such as ING Direct, Fortis Investments, Commerzbank Ag, Royal Bank of Scotland plc, (RBS), and Lloyds.

In the case of Spain, bailed-out banks were smaller in size on an individual basis but were significant in terms of overall market share affected, as some seven banking groups, consolidated from almost thirty former savings banks, have been bailed out and applied state aid rules. These include the imposition of severe downsizing—in terms of business lines, branches, and staff—as well as limitations to retail deposit growth and on interest paid on them.

In the long term, the return of rescued banks to full private ownership and management, or perhaps the liquidation of some of them, will end up restoring competition and opening growth opportunities for those banks that show financial strength and have a proven track record of excellence in customer service.

Direct injection of public capital in problem banks has not been the only tool used by authorities to help banking systems overcome the crisis. There is another one offered to all banks in the system, as it involves the setting up of expansionary monetary policies, with almost unlimited liquidity facilities for banks at virtually zero interest rates. The benefits of such a measure are larger for those banks, or banking systems, with heavier reliance on central bank liquidity as a structural funding source.

Nowhere has such a reliance been more relevant than in the Eurozone, especially since mid-2011, when several European countries (Greece, Ireland, Portugal, Spain, Italy) saw their public debt markets and wholesale banking funding virtually collapse, forcing the European Central Bank (ECB) to facilitate banks' unlimited medium-term (three-year maturity) financing at close to zero interest rate. This financing was made available by using as collateral Treasury bonds subscribed by banks in the primary issuance markets.

This type of ECB facility had two direct consequences. First, it allowed an indirect financing of European governments by the ECB through the intermediation of banks, therefore circumventing the ECB's prohibition on providing direct financing to governments. Second, it gave banks a new source of income through the so-called "carry trade," whereby they get an important margin between the interest received from their Treasury bond portfolios and the virtually zero interest paid on their ECB drawings. Banks in euro countries have made an intense use of those ECB facilities, giving an important push to their net interest margin.

This additional source of net interest income is probably behind the apparent paradox that emerges from Table 3-4. Drawing on BIS data, we have summarized the behavior of net interest income in different banking systems, comparing the average before the crisis (2000 to 2007) and after the crisis started (average 2008 through 2012, latest date available). Eurozone banking systems display an increase in net interest margin contrasting with other banking systems, where net interest margins are clearly below their precrisis levels.

We clearly believe that net interest margin increase in the Eurozone is a temporary exception that will sooner or later be corrected, when the ECB starts retreating from its full allotment facilities. On the contrary, the general trend in banking will be toward further downward pressure on net interest margins everywhere as competition increases, either from new banks being created without legacies from the past, or from other industries (retail, among others) moving into the basic banking business, as we analyze later in the chapter.

In addition to competitive pressures, another important depressing factor on net interest income is the low level of interest rates expected for a long period of time in most developed countries, in an environment of low growth and low inflation expectations. Low-interest-rate environments are prone to depress banks' net interest margin due to the leverage factor exerted by sight deposits. These deposits represent an important part of banks' liabilities. In some cases, especially at banks with a wide penetration in low-income segments of the population, they may account for 30 percent of total liabilities—and are usually paid zero interest, especially small amount sight deposits held as working balances by households and small firms. The contribution of these structural zero-cost deposits is larger in high-interest-rate environments, as these deposits are used to lend at higher interest rates. On the contrary, in low-interest-rate environments, as the one we expect for a long period of time, the contribution of cheap sight deposit is significantly lower.

Taking for granted a structural trend toward lower net interest income, banks should focus on adjusting their cost structure accordingly. This is what emerges from the last columns of Table 3-4, summarizing the behavior of operating costs before and after the crisis. Banking systems have seen their operating costs fall. In fact, cost cutting generally has been more intense than the fall in interest margins, therefore improving the structural efficiency ratio as measured by operational expenses as a fraction of interest margin.

The most significant cases in this regard are Spain, the U.K., and the U.S. among developed markets, as well as Brazil and Russia, all

Table 3-4. Profitability of Major Banks (As a Percentage of Total Assets)

Country	Net interest margin		Loan loss provisions		Operating costs	
	2000-2007	2008-2012	2000-2007	2008-2012	2000-2007	2008-2012
Australia	1.96	1.82	0.19	0.27	1.99	1.20
Canada	1.74	1.61	0.24	0.23	2.73	1.82
France	0.81	0.93	0.13	0.23	1.60	1.08
Germany	0.68	0.82	0.18	0.15	1.38	1.22
Italy	1.69	1.76	0.40	0.78	2.27	1.73
Japan	1.03	0.88	0.56	0.13	0.99	0.80
Spain	2.04	2.34	0.37	1.15	2.29	1.66
Sweden	1.25	0.93	0.05	0.14	1.34	0.85
Switzerland	0.64	0.56	0.05	0.04	2.39	1.92
United Kingdom	1.75	1.11	0.31	0.47	2.02	1.31
United States	2.71	2.44	0.45	0.82	3.58	3.03
Brazil	6.56	4.60	1.24	1.44	6.21	3.56
China	2.74	2.36	0.31	0.28	1.12	1.02
India	2.67	2.63	0.88	0.53	2.48	2.39
Russia	4.86	4.40	0.84	1.13	4.95	2.75

Source: Afi, Analistas Financieros Internacionales, S.A., based on BIS *Annual Report, June 2013*

of which faced large provisioning due to deeper asset deterioration. Japan and Germany, however, faced much smaller asset damage, and their banks have not reduced their operational costs by any significant measure.

These asymmetric behaviors offer important lessons for the competitive positioning of banks in the new landscape after the crisis. To the extent that banking models will only be sustainable if they rest on structural efficiency gains, banks must respond to the market pressure arising from asset-cleaning needs in order to get structural efficiency improvements.

BANK VALUATION DRIVERS

In the new banking environment, in which capital will be scarce and its optimization will be central to strategic decision making, bank valuation becomes paramount because it will become the main lever for raising new capital. In order to explore this issue, we conducted an analysis of the drivers of bank valuation for a sample of ninety large international banks from the U.S., Europe, and Asia. We used the price-to-book ratio (P/B) as the indicator of value, and as explanatory factors we focused on the solvency ratio (measured by Tier 1 capital), profitability (return on equity), and size (market capitalization). We have performed the statistical analysis for two different years, 2007 and 2012, to avoid any biases derived from different time frames related to crisis recovery across different geographical areas.

Looking at the first factor, solvency ratio (measured by Tier 1 capital), the statistical relationship to relative valuation is somewhat ambiguous. In fact, in 2007 there was no relationship. The analysis for 2013 displays a positive relationship, though an extremely poor one in terms of explanatory power. A closer look at differences across geographical areas, however, allows us to conclude that in Asian banks there is no apparent relationship between solvency and valuation; U.S. and European banks, however, display a more positive and significant relationship between solvency and valuation. This is probably a consequence of U.S. and European banks having suffered more adversely the effects of the crisis, with virtual equity dilution in some banks, therefore leading to higher investors' concerns on the availability of higher capital buffers.

Profitability, measured by return on equity (ROE), is certainly a more powerful explanatory factor on relative bank valuation, and this has clearly increased from 2007 (explanatory power of 44 percent) to 2013 (66 percent explanatory power). Banks displaying

Figure 3-4. Bank Valuation (Price-to-Book) and Solvency (Tier 1 Capital)

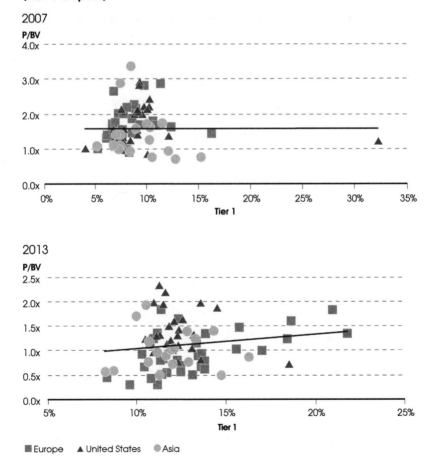

Source: Afi, Analistas Financieros Internacionales, S.A., based on data from Bloomberg L.P.

a ROE of 8 percent are valued at a P/B of approximately 1.0; a ROE of about 5 percent corresponds to a valuation of around 0.8; and a ROE of 12 percent of about 1.5. The strong relationship between ROE and P/B seems to hold with a similar intensity when one looks separately at U.S., European, and Asian banks.

Finally, bank size measured by market cap is not a good predictor of bank valuation, as the statistical relationship between both variables is positive but not significant.

When the three factors are considered simultaneously on a multiple regression framework, only profitability and solvency remain

Figure 3-5. Bank Valuation (Price-to-Book) and Profitability (ROE)

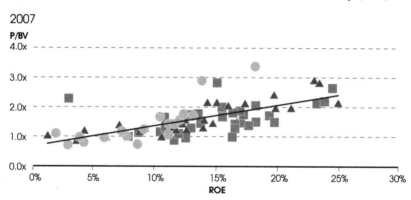

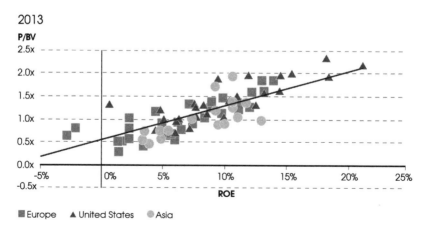

Source: Afi, Analistas Financieros Internacionales, S.A., based on data from Bloomberg L.P.

Figure 3-6. Bank Valuation (Price-to-Book) and Bank Size (Market Cap)

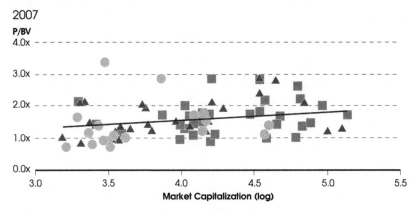

2007

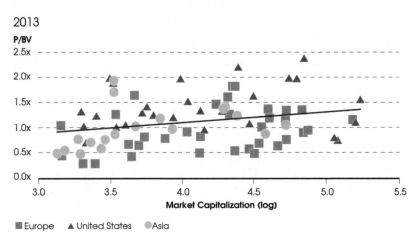

2013

■ Europe　▲ United States　● Asia

Source: Afi, Analistas Financieros Internacionales, S.A., based on data from Bloomberg L.P.

significant (solvency only marginally), while size does not appear significant at all. It follows from here that size by itself is not perceived by the markets as adding value to banks. Some large banks would be more valuable if they jettisoned underperforming business lines.

The Bank of England's Andrew Haldane[4] arrives at the same conclusion, arguing that markets are sending a very clear message to bank managers. Regardless of structural reforms (Vickers, Volcker, Liikanen), markets are telling banks that they should separate activities and concentrate only on those creating value: if banks are priced at less than book, shareholders would prefer to sell the various assets within the bank separately.

A similar conclusion is reached by a recent McKinsey report on restructuring pressures for international banks: "Financial institutions must build critical mass in their core businesses and divest subscale, noncore, and capital-consuming operations. Consequently, there will be a shift toward scale and to having business lines run by their best natural owner."[5]

From all of these arguments we can arrive at some forward-looking conclusions regarding bank size and complexity: Whether or not regulation is effective in forcing the breakup of large and complex banking organization, it seems clear that market forces and pressure to rebuild profitability will lead banks to focus on what they can do best, and therefore be in a better competitive position that they can exploit.

Banks will need to shed assets and business lines that are no longer profitable at the level of equity required, and instead concentrate on profitable business lines. Banks, however, will find ample room for economies of scale within the business lines they decide to keep; not only in terms of cost savings but especially in terms of information management and offering value to customers.

ECONOMIES OF SCALE IN BANKING

The benefits of size in banking are mainly related to the existence of economies of scale that reduce unit operating costs. Size can also enhance the ability of banks to realize economies of scope, as large banks are more likely to achieve scope in multiple activities while at the same time maintaining scale in each individual activity.

Early empirical analysis of economies of scale in banking found limited scale economies, which tended to peak at relatively low levels of assets. Studies by Allen Berger and Loretta Mester[6] found that economies of scale in banking got exhausted at moderate levels of assets, as long as the average cost curve has a relatively flat U-shape with medium-sized firms being slightly more scale efficient than either very large or very small firms.

Compensating for pure scale diseconomies beyond a certain size threshold, previous studies have also emphasized the distortion introduced by "too big to fail" considerations. Big banks, perceived to be more protected than the rest, would enjoy a clear advantage in the deposit market, translating into lower financing costs. Andrew Haldane[7] estimates the implicit subsidy that big banks enjoy, and finds that it accounts for most of the economies of scale observed among the large banks. He performs an estimation taking out the implicit subsidy (charging large banks the extra funding cost they would face in the absence of implicit guarantees), and concludes that economies of scale completely disappear (see Figure 3-7).

There is no consensus on this point, however. In a recent study Loretta Mester and Joseph Hughes[8] conclude that greater economies of scale exist, beyond those created by higher bank sizes, than was traditionally believed, and beyond the subsidy implicit in "too big to fail" considerations. They arrive at such conclusions by using more flexible production models that allow managers to design the business model most appropriate for an optimal risk-return combination, instead of pure minimum cost production function.

Their results indicate that economies of scale are not a result of the cost advantages large banks may derive from "too big to fail" (TBTF) considerations. Instead, they follow from technological advantages, such as diversification and the spreading of information costs and other costs that do not increase proportionately with size. Significant economies of scale in banking suggest that technological factors, as well as TBTF cost advantages, appear to have been an important driver of banks' increasing size.

Looking forward, and considering the new capital surcharges that will be imposed on systemic banks, it seems that TBTF advantages will mostly disappear. From here it seems that the only drivers for bank size will rest on economies of scale, and these certainly

Figure 3-7. Economies of Scale in Banking: The effect of "Too-big-to-fail" subsidy

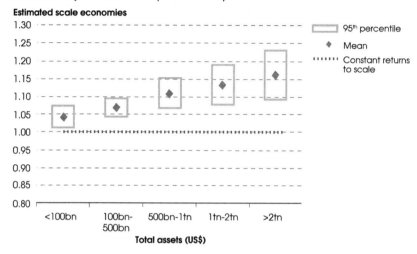

Without adjustment for implicit subsidy

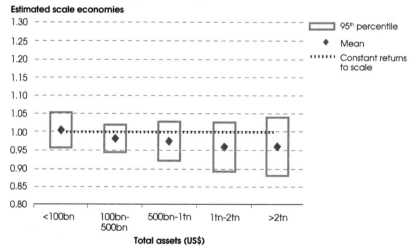

With adjustment for implicit subsidy

Source: Bank of England´s Andrew Haldane: On being the right size. Speech at Institute of Economic Affairs' 22nd Annual Series, The 2012 Beesley Lectures at the Institute of Directors, Pall Mall, October 25, 2012

exist. This will be especially true under a new banking paradigm in which customer management will rest less on relationship banking and more on hard information processing.

INDUSTRY CONVERGENCE, CUSTOMER LOYALTY, AND TECHNOLOGY

Technology has already transformed many industries, and so it is going to do with the banking industry, exposing it to much more intense competition not only from existing banks but from new entrants, in a clear movement of industry convergence. Technology is going to change competition in banking in at least two ways: there will be more flexibility for customers to move from one bank to another, thereby reducing customer loyalty; the erosion of customer loyalty will make "hard" information about customers more valuable, to the detriment of "soft" information on which traditional relationship banking was based.

Customer switching has a lot to do with loyalty, and customer loyalty toward banks is currently far from optimal. According to TNS Global, a leading political and social research company,[9] banks command one of the lowest levels of customer satisfaction and loyalty, higher only than utilities, and clearly worse than other industries like mobile operators, automobiles, and supermarkets, the highest ranked in customer loyalty.

Satisfaction and loyalty to banks are even worse among the young population (eighteen- to thirty-four-year-olds): almost three-quarters of them think there are no differences between banks, and those people are four times more likely to switch than the average bank customer. In fact, according to the same TNS study, actual switching among bank customers is much smaller than the desire to switch, because of both inconvenience and a bank's market power.

In such an environment, a truly game-changing disruption in banking competition is going to come from efforts to facilitate customer switching across banks. Some countries, like the U.S. and

Australia, started some time ago to move in this direction, with requirements on banks to make more information available for customers. More recently, in 2013, the U.K.'s Financial Conduct Authority (FCA) has been especially committed to implementing a new current account redirection service to enhance the process for individuals and small businesses who wish to switch to a new provider. The FCA proposal, to which thirty-three banks covering more than 97 percent of the current account market adhered, was to reach a seven-day switching service by the end of 2013. The new switching service guarantees that the switch to the new account happens within seven working days of opening the new account, is free to use for the customer, catches all credits and debits into the old (closed) account for a period of thirteen months, sends reminders to direct debit originators to update the details on their systems, and provides a guarantee that customers will not suffer any loss if mistakes occur.

Recently published results by the Payments Council[10] on the performance of the new service during its first three months of activity point to a clear success, as far as it has increased the public awareness of the new service; and target performance has been reached, as 99.6 percent of the switching processes started by customers were completed in seven working days, as committed by the adhered banks. Switching activity has also increased by 17 percent on a year over year basis, when considered a full quarter (fourth quarter 2013); but by 54 percent when the last month (December) was compared with the same month one year earlier. Given the success of the new service, the U.K. government may not feel the need to consider more radical alternatives, one of them being full bank account number portability (BANP).

A generalization of these switching facilities will no doubt put downward pressure on customers' loyalty toward incumbent banks, making it easier for other banks (existing or newly created) or even other industry operators to capture discontented customers. Among these other operators, retailers pose the most immediate threats to traditional banks. Retail is among the industries with the highest customer satisfaction and loyalty, and it has withstood the ravages of the recession, making retailers especially appropriate to benefit from banks' loss of customer loyalty. Some of the major and most recognized retailers are already competing on retail financial services such as credit cards and lending, and are progressively moving toward opening current accounts, as Marks & Spencer plc and Tesco PLC, have already announced they will do.

Traditional retailers are not the only threat to incumbent banks; there is also the possibility of new banks that have minimum infrastructure investments and a flexible cost structure. The U.K.'s Metro Bank plc, launched in 2010, is a clear example in this sense. By operating an IT platform (supplied by Temenos) under a monthly subscription based on the number of customers in the business, Metro Bank was able to get licensed, set up and open a small number of branches, and perform basic banking services at extremely favorable conditions for customers, and with a low and flexible cost structure. A quite similar example is Aldermore, also run on a rented IT platform and under a hybrid (own and white-labeled) product provision, especially focused on commercial and SME customers. These are just two examples of a model that is expected to grow everywhere.

As BBVA Chairman Francisco Gonzalez recently wrote, "new entrants are free from the legacies of obsolete banks: obsolete systems and costly distribution networks. So far, most of these new entrants (PayPal Pte. Ltd., Square, Inc., iZettle AB, Sum Up Advisory Inc., Dwolla, Inc.) are seen as niche businesses. However, they may expand or seek alliances. And almost certainly some big names in the digital world, companies with strong brands and millions of users, will jump into the fray."[11]

For banks, this represents both an opportunity and a threat. Numerous new competitors are coming up with innovations in the digital banking space. In the process, they are eating away at parts of the banking value chain. Google Inc., has launched a plastic debit card to accompany its Google Wallet™, which is used by millions of consumers, and PayPal is the number one online payment method in many countries. The risk for banks is that these new digital competitors will consign them to a limited role as utilities that provide only basic banking services to customers.

By contrast, banks have a unique opportunity to use digital communications tools to capitalize on the significant advantage they have at their disposal, chiefly information about consumer transactions and spending habits. By combining this data with personalized information from other sources such as social media, they have the chance to provide a valuable service to clients when they are making transactions. In time, almost all banks will be able to provide tailored advertising and offers to customers by mobile, and using big (hard) data will allow banks to price properly for customer wallet share. These offerings, indeed, will be most supportive for the larger banks: the more data, the better.

THE TALENT WAR IN BANKING

Changes in the banking business model derived from greater technology intensity, much higher standards of customer service, and ease of entry into the market by new banks will create a competitive environment in which only the best will survive; the need for excellent employees will never have been greater.

The war for talent in banking coincides with a regulatory agenda emphasizing new rules and limitations on compensation. Prior to the crisis, pay levels in banking for executives and certain other employees rose much more quickly than in other parts of the economy. Moreover, there is a general belief that compensation policies in banking have contributed to excessive risk taking. This is why one of the first mandates the Financial Stability Board received from the G20 leaders was to develop sound practices on bank compensation.

The most ambitious and far-reaching study on bank compensation relative to other business sectors is by Thomas Philippon and Ariell Reshef,[12] which covered an entire century. According to this study, wages in banking were more than 1.5 times greater than in the nonfinancial sectors in the early twentieth century, coming down very quickly in the wake of the Great Depression, and leveling off during the 1960s and '70s. Over the last four decades they have reached an even higher level at a multiplier of 1.7.

The study's most significant finding, however, is the close relationship that relative wages in banking have with two significant factors; namely, regulation and employee qualifications (measured by the share of employees with higher-education degrees). It is not hard to come up with an explanatory argument for these simultaneous correlations. When deregulation is higher, banks are able to engage in more diverse and more complex activities, in contrast with the simpler, more traditional, and less demanding intermediation activities.

While this relationship between deregulation and relative education is clear, and it should translate into higher relative salaries according to the complexity of activities as well as the higher educational credentials required, questions arise about the perverse incentives between payment policies and excessive risk taking. From a regulatory point of view, bank compensation policies should not be relevant in terms of absolute or even relative terms, but only to the extent that they create incentives for excessive risk taking.

Future trends in recruiting and compensation policies in banking will be conditioned by regulatory pressures, as well as competitive forces shaping the new landscape after the crisis. Banks should expect an increase in the overall level of regulation, and stock market pressures will likely induce banks to step back from riskier activities and focus instead on a narrower set of businesses. These two forces will tend to reduce the excess payments that bank employees, especially those involved in riskier activities like investment banking, have enjoyed during the last three decades relative to other sectors of the economy. A decrease in consumer trust in the industry, together with constrained incentivization, may lower the attraction of a career in banking for new graduates and experienced talent alike.

At the same time, however, there will be a new type of war for talent in activities centered on extracting value from big data on customers as well as on exploiting the potential of new technologies in gaining access to broader segments of customers. The changing nature of work and competition from digital businesses for the best talent will lead banks not just to reconsider how to attract talent, it will cause them to contemplate whole new employment models.

A combination of these opposing forces—regulatory downward pressure on compensation and a talent war—will lead to wider pay ranges inside banks, with a more accurate link to performance, and also toward incorporating risk-adjusted metrics in performance measurement and incentives.

DISINTERMEDIATION TRENDS AND COMPETITION

The banking industry is also going to be transformed by the emergence of alternative forms of financial intermediation, from shadow banking to peer-to-peer lending. New forms of finance are maturing at the same time that the structure and activities of traditional banks are under scrutiny. Some of those new finance alternatives, like shadow banking, emerge mainly as a way to eliminate regulations or limitations to traditional banking. Others, like peer-to-peer lending or crowdfunding—new developments facilitated by social networks—are keeping banks from performing their lending function for specific borrowers. One way or another, the emergence of new forms of finance outside the traditional intermediation channel is going to affect the competitive structure of banking everywhere.

Shadow Banking

An important factor in shaping the new competitive structure in banking has to do with the evolution of shadow banking and, more generally, the nonbanking ways of channeling funds from savers to borrowers. All these alternative funding schemes will evolve in a double loop with traditional bank intermediation activities. On the one hand, they will grow as an answer to demands from customers that will not be supplied by traditional banking. On the other, there is the temptation to perform some traditional activities under shadow banking, if new bank regulation maintains, or even increases, the scope for regulatory arbitrage between both types of banking. For example, the new Basel III framework may create further incentives for banks to try to avoid higher risk weights and capital requirements through securitization, or to avoid limitations to leverage by investing in nonbank financial institutions with high leverage to obtain a higher return on equity.

Shadow banking has often been mentioned as one of the main factors behind the crisis, or at least an accelerant, due to its opaque and unregulated nature. This has raised increasing concerns about potential contamination of traditional regulated banking. It was this concern that led the G20 leaders at the Seoul meeting in 2010 (the same that paved the way for Basel III) to request that the Financial Stability Board (FSB) develop a body of recommendations on oversight and regulation of shadow banking all over the world.

Shadow banking refers to activities related to credit intermediation, liquidity, and maturity transformation that take place outside the regulated banking system. As such, it is difficult to define shadow banking other than by exclusion, but it is generally accepted that its main constituents are securitization entities, relevant for the asset side of financial intermediation, and money market funds (MMF), hedge funds (HF), securities lending (SL), and repo broker-dealers, relevant for the funding side of banks.

According to the FSB,[13] shadow banking registered very high growth rates in all jurisdictions before the crisis, but it has since decelerated in most of them, China being the main exception. In particular, securitization markets remained impaired in most regions and segments, and MMFs suffered from the prolonged period of very low interest rates, which put their business model at risk. In fact, according to the FSB, if one proxies the shadow banking system by "other financial intermediaries," its share of total financial intermediation has decreased since the onset of the crisis and recently has been stable at a level of about 25 percent of the total financial system, after having peaked at 27 percent in 2007.

From a financial stability viewpoint, however, more important than the size of shadow banking itself is the interconnectedness between shadow and formal banking systems, as this can create systemic risks. These risks may arise not only from cross-asset and liability positions between both types of banking systems, but also from common exposure to the same sectors of activity. Problems in shadow banking could contaminate the formal banking sector, as both are subject to the same financial imperatives and sensitivities regarding the economic cycle; in fact, they can lead to an increase in pro-cyclicality or even exacerbate liquidity problems.

According to the FSB, such interconnectedness creates risks that are higher for shadow banks than for formal banks in most of the countries covered in its analysis. As Figure 3-8 shows, while banks' dependency on OFIs, either on the asset or liability side, represents less than 20 percent of total banks' assets, the figures are more than double when analyzed from the viewpoint of OFIs: their relationship with formal banking represents a bigger share of their total assets.

Potential for further growth in the shadow banking system will rest on the relative regulatory burden between "official" and "shadow" banking. We tend to believe that, as long as shadow banking is broadly defined and covers many different activities, it will always be possible to find loopholes in which to develop some financial activities subject to lower regulatory burdens.

Shadow Banking: The Special Case of China

Nowhere is the relationship between shadow banking development and the extent of regulation in the formal banking sector as clear as it is in China. The explosive growth registered in China's shadow banking system, and the opacity surrounding it, is one of the main factors that triggered recent calls for stricter regulation and transparency.

To start with, it is hard to define shadow banking in China, more

Figure 3-8. Banks' Assets and Liabilities to Nonbank Financial Intermediaries (at End of 2011)

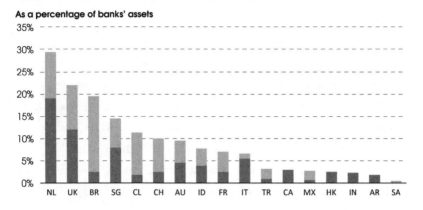

As a percentage of banks' assets

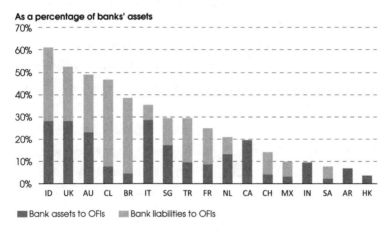

As a percentage of banks' assets

■ Bank assets to OFIs   ■ Bank liabilities to OFIs

AR = Argentina; AU = Australia; BR = Brazil; CA = Canada; CH = Switzerland; CL = Chile; FR = France; HK = Hong Kong; ID = Indonesia; IN = India; IT = Italy; MX = Mexico; NL = Netherlands; SA = Saudi Arabia; SG = Singapore; TR = Turkey; UK = United Kingdom.

Note: Liabilities of banks to OFIs are not available for Argentina, Canada, Hong Kong, and India.

Source: Afi, Analistas Financieros Internacionales, S.A., based on FSB *Global Shadow Banking Monitoring Report 2012*

so than in any other country. The largest segment is related to trust companies that invest clients' money according to some investment objectives (maturity, instruments, etc.) and wealth management products that have been developed as a way to avoid Chinese limitations on deposit remuneration. Bank deposits are capped at 110 percent of the benchmark rates set by the Central Bank. By the end of 2013, these benchmark rates stood at 3 percent for deposit taking and 6 percent for lending.

Eager to get returns in excess of those capped rates, Chinese investors have flooded certain wealth management vehicles (somewhat similar to money market funds, but much less regulated than in the U.S. or Europe) with money. Total assets under management are estimated at some 15 trillion yuan ($2.5 trillion), equivalent to almost 30 percent of China's GDP. With such large sums at play, the main worry behind China's shadow banking system is the risk of default on the part of borrowers of those investment funds, as well as the extent to which the Chinese government ultimately guarantees the borrowing. While this type of risk is not very different from the one being borne by investors in MMF in many other countries, the problem in China may be that many investors implicitly believe that the government, or the banks, will be acting as a backstop in case of default on the underlying projects.

Public confidence in implicit government support for some risky investments made in the shadow banking system may have recently been reaffirmed by the handling of what was feared to be one of the largest failures in the unregulated Chinese financial system. A 3 billion yuan ($500 million) investment product named "Credit Equals Gold #1" issued in 2011 by China Credit Trust (CCT), one of the country's biggest shadow banks, was expected to go bankrupt by the time of maturity on January 31, 2014, as the mining company (Zhenfu Energy Group Ltd.) serving as collateral for the product had been in trouble for the previous two years. The product didn't fail as anticipated, due to a third party who purchased the underlying investment and reduced the loss faced by initial investors.[14] There was likely an implicit bailout in order to avoid a disorderly disruption of the entire shadow banking system. Moreover, as important as avoiding a disorderly disruption of the Chinese shadow banking system, one must also take into serious consideration the need to introduce some discipline and fear of losses so that investors cannot assume that they can obtain extra returns without incurring extra risks. The Central Bank has been trying to apply the brakes, or at least to establish controls, on the growth of these unregulated vehicles. It is, however, unlikely that these controls or limitations will get to the point of eliminating a source of funding that is currently the only one available for many financially restricted private firms or even local governments.

A more rational possibility might be to act on the true causes of shadow banking's explosive growth—rate limitations on the regulated banking system. This is probably the road Chinese authorities will take in the medium term.

In the short term, however, such a measure is not to be expected, as it would put tremendous pressure on the largest regulated banks, whose profitability rests mostly on the current rate limitation. The official ceiling on deposit rates allows Chinese banks to enjoy a cheap source of funding that gives them a competitive advantage relative to banks in the rest of the world. Three of the four largest Chinese banks—ICBC, China Construction Bank, and Agricultural Bank of China—generated in 2012 twice as much interest income as Citigroup and JPMorgan Chase.

The high profitability of the largest Chinese banks is part of the ammunition that allows them to be used as the main lever to implement the stimulus packages orchestrated by the government in the last three years. For Chinese regulators this raises some considerable risks; their final resolution will shape the future banking industry in the largest and arguably most promising market in the world.

If the ceiling is eliminated, big banks risk losing most of their competitive advantage, and, in the event of loan losses increasing sharply, risk getting short of capital. If the ceiling is maintained to protect those large "official" banks, incentives will remain for even faster growth in shadow banking. This dilemma, however and whenever it is solved, is key to the competitive dynamic in the Chinese market, and therefore for opportunities for global banks to position themselves in that market.

Nonbank SME Finance

Small and medium-sized companies (SMEs) have been especially hard hit since the crisis began. They have traditionally faced difficulties in accessing appropriate funding to grow. As SMEs are overly reliant on bank financing, they have suffered especially from finance scarcity in a context where crisis-hit banks have been forced to deleverage. The situation is especially worrying in European countries, where SMEs' bank reliance is much more acute than it is in the U.S. or U.K.

Some initiatives to push new forms of nonbank SME finance have been promoted by European authorities. Among these are new frameworks for investment in venture capital. Some policy initiatives have also been promoted to facilitate SMEs' access to equity markets. Proposals have also been presented to allow the operators of multilateral trading platforms to be registered under the label of "SME growth market."

Besides these new forms of finance promoted by the European authorities, however, private initiatives are growing up around new financing sources especially suited for SMEs. Among these a prominent place has to be given to crowdfunding, which benefits from social networks, and which enables the easy diffusion of information about new business ideas. The result is that those who want to borrow are matched with those who want to lend, keeping banks out of the game.

Fund solicitation through the Internet, for the provision of financial resources to support specific purposes or projects, constitutes the essence of crowdfunding. Resources can be solicited in the form of a donation or in exchange for some type of return, either fixed or linked to project success. According to this range, one may distinguish two different types of crowdfunding: nonfinancial (basically tied to donations and/or rewards in the form of presales and the like) and pure financial crowdfunding, either debt or equity finance.

The recent rise in crowdfunding can be explained with purely economic arguments: matching funders with creators or project developers is now more efficient and effective due to lower search costs online; and low communication costs facilitate better information gathering and progress monitoring for distant funders, therefore allowing funders to participate in the development of the idea.

All this makes crowdfunding an interesting concept with a promising future within the nonfinancial category, as long as it encourages innovation, raising awareness, and building communities. Though it represents a form of nonbank finance, and therefore is a threat to banks' role in financial markets, crowdfunding also presents opportunities for banks because it acts as a subsequent accelerator for bank lending: banks are more likely to lend money if the project is already being funded through a platform.

Crowdfunding has attracted many different business models that make it more difficult to regulate on a comprehensive basis. In fact, crowdfunding practices cut across different types of regulations, including market infrastructure, payment systems, e-commerce, and so on, opening up the opportunity to develop a more horizontal approach to investor protection. Despite these uncertainties regarding future crowdfunding regulation, new online platforms, peer-to-peer (P2P) funders, and crowd funders could seize a small but significant share of the market for SME finance.

CONCLUSION: A NEW COMPETITIVE LANDSCAPE

The global banking business is going to face dramatic change in the competitive landscape. It would be extremely simple to attribute that change entirely to the crisis, or to the different decisions that governments have adopted to cope with it. In fact, the biggest factor of change is tied to deep, underlying structural trends—demographic, sociological, technological, and so on—and the financial crisis simply imposes on banks a much faster speed of adjustment in their business models to cope with these changes.

Most developed countries show clear symptoms of excess banking capacity, leading to downward pressures on margins and profitability. This trend, together with higher capital requirements and difficulty raising new capital from markets, will lead most banks to optimize scarce capital by focusing on those business lines where they can attain better returns on required capital. This trend is also supported by market valuation parameters, which no longer are supportive of size as a competitive advantage by itself.

On the contrary, market valuation is mostly related to bank profitability, as well as to banks' financial health. This raises an apparent paradox, as long as banks' profitability is highly dependent on finding new growth avenues, which should be supported by increased lending; but this will only be possible for those banks able to credibly promise to investors adequate return on their investments in capital.

Emerging markets present better growth opportunities for banks than developed ones. Some of them, however, display a combination—fast economic growth, intense competition, excessive credit expansion, and weak regulation standards—that is likely to produce a banking environment vulnerable to risks of bubbles. This is why banks with a global scope should expand selectively, either following their existing customers as they go overseas or choosing demographic segments in which they can leverage their domestic competitive advantages. The competitive environment for banking will also be deeply changed by an array of technological developments ranging from mass consumer adoption of digital and mobile social technologies to advances around customer data and analytics.

The effects of these technological developments on banking competition will be amplified by regulatory incentives to facilitate switching of customers across different banks, or even to new entrants in the banking industry. These new entrants do not have the legacy deadweights that many banks incorporate—in terms of fixed costs, but also in terms of customer dissatisfaction and lost loyalty— while they can easily replicate basic banking operations with flexible cost structures.

However, banks have an opportunity to respond to this threat by leveraging the vast amount of data they have about their customers and combining it with personalized information from other sources such as social media in order to provide a valuable service to clients when they are making transactions.

Pay and recruiting policies in banking will be strongly conditioned by regulatory pressures and by competitive forces shaping the new industry landscape. An increase in the overall level of regulation, pressures to step back from riskier activities, and a focus on a narrower approach to bank competitiveness will reduce the excessive compensation that bank employees have enjoyed during the last three decades relative to other sectors of the economy. At the same time, there will be a new war for talent in activities centered on extracting value from big data on customers as well as on exploiting the potential of new technologies in gaining access to broader segments of clients.

CHAPTER 4

Legitimacy

Among the most pervasive effects of the global financial crisis, the sudden decline in the legitimacy of banks stands out as perhaps one of the most persistent and intractable problems. Banks, while oftentimes admired, have never been loved by the public; bankers even less so. At the same time, banks cannot possibly operate without being perceived as legitimate agents in the financial services sector. At the core of the problem lies the basic fact that banks are the depositories of the public's trust. Banks, to play a role in the modern economy, need the unmitigated confidence of the public in what they do and how they go about doing it.

Society is asking many questions about the role that banks play in the economy in general, and about their contribution to societal well-being in particular. The focus on shareholder value is being attacked not only as unfair to other stakeholders but as potentially detrimental to the economy, given that banks act as a crucial nexus between the providers of capital and those who need it for consumption and investment. At the same time, banks have been accused of lack of transparency and of abusive practices toward customers. Moreover, banks are now being asked to pursue a social agenda when it comes to credit allocation and financial inclusion, contributing to creating social value in ways that may or may not contribute to their profitability.

The legitimacy of banks has suffered along three distinct dimensions. The first is a decline in the trust that the public, government officials, and regulators have traditionally placed in the banks. The second has manifested itself as a criticism of compensation levels and systems for bankers, traders, and other bank employees. The entire model of corporate governance has been called into question. The third has to do with the decline in customer loyalty. Let us analyze each in turn.

LACK OF TRUST

Banks are peculiar institutions, as they are built on trust. Savers, depositors, investors, borrowers, and people or businesses making payments need banks. As one seasoned banker confided to us, "Banks are different from any other type of company in that they are always technically bankrupt, even when they are operating normally." This is the case because they typically make loans far in excess of the deposit base or the assets they possess. In order to leverage themselves, banks need to develop trust in their business model.

There is a tremendous degree of heterogeneity in terms of the trust that the public places in individual banks. Some have a very strong reputation for the solidity and strength of their balance sheet while others have less. Regardless of such differences, however, banking crises tend to affect banks in a more general way. And the problem is that banking crises have become very common since the 1970s. The recent global financial crisis was primarily a banking crisis. Even after it mutated into a sovereign debt crisis, banks around the world have continued to suffer from a much lower level of trust than was placed in them before the crisis started. The crisis has effectively made the public much more skeptical about the role of banks in the economy and about their ways of doing business.

Surveys show that the general public's trust in banks and the banking sector is at a level of about half of where it was before the crisis, especially in Western Europe and the United States. There are twice as many bank customers globally who disagree or strongly disagree that they have trust and confidence in the banking industry as those who agree or strongly agree. The lack of trust is most pronounced in parts of the world in which financial volatility is higher (e.g., Latin America, the Middle East, Africa). It is also interesting to see that trust in banks is lower in the United States than it is in Europe, although the credit crunch seems to be more severe in the latter.[1]

The trust problem facing banks is even more readily apparent when it comes to investors. Many solid and profitable banks around the world are still trading below book value or only slightly above it. Back in 2009 and 2010, most bank stocks traded below. Any premium above tangible book value, of course, has to be justified by profitability in excess of the cost of equity. In many cases, however, profitability is not the issue; it is risk. Equity markets continue to see bank stocks as inherently risky and volatile, especially those of large banks. In the future, banks will also need to address investors' lack of confidence.

Banks would be wise to address their deteriorating trust by keeping some important principles in mind:

- The decline in trust should not be framed exclusively as a public relations problem. Banks may have a PR problem as well, but there is something more fundamental that needs to be fixed to reverse the erosion of trust than pure window dressing.

- Banks need to design a comprehensive approach to rebuilding trust, one focused on a transformation of the fundamental ways of doing business in the area of risk management and on a more comprehensive approach to stakeholder-aligned management and corporate governance.

• Rebuilding trust requires the attention of the top management team and its commitment to changing aspects of the business model that will make outside parties (customers, investors, the surrounding community, and the general public) more at ease with the bank and its operations.

• Changing some of the technical and hard factors that impact trust, such as product and fee transparency or managerial compensation and incentives, are potential short-term fixes; many soft factors, such as company culture, are harder to change and can only be transformed over a period of years.

These principles will be next to impossible to implement without a different approach to corporate governance, one that more broadly respects the different stakeholders as opposed to privileging one of them. In the near future, banks that fail to address this problem will find themselves at a disadvantage in terms of attracting funding and customers, precisely at a time when new regulations are likely to raise the bar for all banks.

CORPORATE GOVERNANCE, STAKEHOLDER MANAGEMENT, AND SOCIAL RESPONSIBILITY

There is an irony in recent developments concerning corporate governance at financial institutions. In many parts of the world, banks were once faulted for not keeping in mind shareholders when it came to making strategic decisions. As banks became more dependent on the markets for funding, they made considerable efforts to show that their shareholders were put first and that management was their faithful agent. Banks in Europe, Latin America, and much of Asia adopted codes of good governance and overhauled their corporate governance systems to make them more shareholder friendly. Many of them appointed independent directors to the board and published an annual report on corporate governance. The emphasis on shareholder value spread like wildfire in the late 1990s and during the first few years of the twenty-first century, only to come under severe attack in the wake of the financial crisis.

The crisis revealed many different kinds of problems with corporate governance at the banks. One of them had to do with the fact that the rhetoric of shareholder value did not prevent shareholders from suffering big losses. Criticisms mounted after the shareholders and the general public learned that bank executives continued to receive bonuses even when achieving lower levels of financial performance or sustaining outright financial losses.

As incendiary as the issue of executive compensation proved to be, it paled by comparison with the overall perception that banks' corporate governance systems were antiquated and out of touch with the more complex reality of the so-called "stakeholder society." Precisely because banks are such central institutions in the economy, public expectations as to corporate governance are unusually high when it comes to the banking sector. And yet, many banks continue to struggle with how to cope with societal demands for a truly stakeholder-based system of governance and accountability.

The stakeholder view of the firm dates back to the 1960s but did not make the headlines in the United States until the 1980s. This was the time when pundits observed that German and Japanese companies benefited from the consensus and stability generated by managing the firm according to stakeholder principles. The idea that more value could be created by maximizing joint outcomes became popular. Focusing on shareholder wealth alone jeopardized performance by alienating key stakeholders such as employees, who might not work as hard, thus eroding the foundations for superior value creation.

While the initial approaches to stakeholder management focused on ways to engage employees, suppliers, customers, and other constituencies with a view to enhancing value creation, critics noted that the very definition of value needed to be revisited. The idea of "corporate social responsibility" is both about the definition of the value that the company is supposed to create, adding other considerations besides financial performance, and about the process by which the company makes decisions, considering goals other than profitability or shareholder returns.

In most countries banks have historically embraced the simplest way of creating social value by pursuing very ambitious philanthropic agendas. Corporate philanthropy can make a big difference in society, and banks have been at the forefront of such efforts, funding many worthy charitable causes. The crisis, however, has made the public much more demanding, especially when it comes to banks. Philanthropy alone is unlikely to satisfy demands for transparency and social engagement.

In the future, banks will need to reorient their approach to corporate governance and social responsibility:

• Banks will need to strike a new balance among key stakeholders (shareholders, bondholders, employees, customers, and the surrounding community) that reflects their contribution to the bank's financial performance, solidity as a financial institution, and reputation. Macro demographic trends and new regulations are likely to bring about shifts in the relative importance of debt, equity, and deposits, as we analyzed in previous chapters. As a result, banks need to develop the kind of flexibility in their corporate governance systems that will enable them to accommodate such shifting trends.

• Banks need to revamp their philanthropic efforts and turn them into more comprehensive social responsibility programs. Socially responsible investing, community banking, and other similar trends offer ideas for new initiatives that banks could launch in order to add social value and establish a better reputation for themselves.

• For banks, social responsibility must also include profitability, balance-sheet strength, and resilience to crises. Therefore, banks need to more effectively engage all stakeholders when it comes to communicating the need to continue playing their crucial role of lending even during the most difficult times.

• Given banks' increasing reliance on shareholders and bond-holders as crucial sources of funds, they need to better understand that their brand reputation can be enhanced by developing more coherent and comprehensive social responsibility agendas. Such an agenda makes a bank more competitive with customers and employees: survey research indicates that in many markets people prefer to do business with and work for a company with a good reputation for adding social value.

• From the point of view of the customer, banks need to use information to draw a segmentation map of their customer base from the point of view of social responsibility. Customers, including both individuals and small businesses, differ massively when it comes to what they expect the bank to do from a social-value point of view. Some care primarily about seeing the bank help the community by making charitable donations, while others want the bank to be more transparent or to incorporate social-value accounting throughout its organization. It would be a bigger mistake to assume that all customers want the same approach to corporate social responsibility and a stakeholder-oriented mode of corporate governance than to continue emphasizing shareholder value alone. Banks need to map their stakeholders, their values, and their expectations carefully.

• Demands for transparency and a stakeholder-based model of corporate governance will need to go beyond new regulatory requirements if banks wish to rebuild their reputation faster than the competition. For smaller banks, listening to the community may become a differentiator. For larger banks, the ones whose reputation has suffered the most, comprehensive corporate governance changes will be a must.

CRITICISM ABOUT INCENTIVES AND COMPENSATION

The decline in trust faced by banks worldwide has been compounded by revelations about incentives and compensation for top executives, traders, and other bank personnel. There is a widespread public perception that bankers have abused the privileges and perks of the job, often making out like bandits even as their banks sunk or had to be bailed out by taxpayers. The fact that several financial institutions have suffered multibillion-dollar losses, or have even gone bust, as a result of the investments made by small departments or even individual rogue traders has exacerbated the public's perception of a lack of moderation, common sense, and control when it comes to incentives and compensation. Politicians have also seized upon these themes to score points with a public that is disillusioned with financial institutions and demands to know why banks are so prone to failure and have to be bailed out.

In the U.S. there is a long history of attempts to impose salary caps for financial corporations, including banks. During the 1930s early legislative proposals were abandoned, and something similar happened in the wake of the Great Recession of 2008 to 2009. In the end, only companies and banks that received bailout money from the Troubled Assets Relief Program (TARP) were subject to a $500,000 cash limit and the requirement that compensation in the form of options be in restricted stock with some rules for when it could be sold.

One of the most common regulatory responses to executive compensation was to pass "say on pay" legislation, which mandated that compensation guidelines be put to a vote among shareholders of all publicly listed corporations. Since 2002 a number of countries have passed such a rule, including Australia, Denmark, Germany, the Netherlands, Sweden, the U.K., and the U.S. (as part of the Dodd-Frank Act of 2010). However, only in Denmark, the Netherlands, and Sweden is the vote on compensation guidelines binding. Another regulatory response has been to introduce compensation disclosure requirements; this has been done in Australia, France, Germany, the Netherlands, Sweden, and the U.K. In the U.S. such requirements have been on the books since the 1930s.[2] "Say on pay" and disclosure requirements do not necessarily place caps on the amount of executive compensation, nor do they specify the kind of compensation or incentives that can be offered. Rather, they are provisions meant to increase transparency or to perhaps shame executives into limiting their compensation, especially in the U.S., where disclosure of individual compensation has been mandatory for many years.

Given the public's continued discomfort with, if not outrage at, executive compensation, and the potential threat of new regulations, banks would be wise to:

• Reexamine compensation practices for top executives to ensure compliance with new regulations, codes of good governance, and emerging informal norms within the industry.

• Critically reconsider compensation levels, setting them so they are high enough to attract and maintain needed talent but do not become a financial burden on the corporation or a source of discontent on the part of internal and external stakeholders.

• Revisit the composition of executive pay packages and alter them so they avoid situations in which managerial incentives privilege short-term gains at the expense of the long-term health, balance-sheet solidity, and profitability of the bank.

A problem separate from executive compensation has to do with the incentives and pay packages for traders and other employees making investment decisions that can potentially cost the bank billions of dollars, such as those that have affected several U.S. and European financial institutions. "Say on pay" or disclosure regulations do not tend to apply to this kind of employee, but that should be no excuse for banks to neglect the problem. The key issue involves risk management. Banks should reexamine their compensation practices for trades. Most importantly, they must establish more fluid lines of communication and more effective oversight mechanisms so that "rogue" or unauthorized behaviors by one individual cannot put the bank's finances or its reputation at risk. Blaming individual employees for the misdeed, even when outright criminal behavior is involved, in no way exonerates executives and the board of directors from their responsibilities to ensure that the bank's internal procedures are consistent with the risk management practices and safeguards that must be in place in any modern financial institution.

More generally, the new political and popular attention given to compensation and incentives requires not only compliance with new regulations but a more systematic effort by banks to be in tune with social demands and expectations. Banks cannot view popular dissatisfaction with their compensation practices as an isolated issue. It is one that may end up affecting their entire operation in at least two ways. We have already analyzed the first, that is, the impact of compensation and incentives on risk management systems and practices. The second has to do with customer loyalty, especially in a context in which smaller banks and nonbank institutions stand to win customers if large banks continue to give the impression that high levels of compensation are more important than customer satisfaction. We turn to this topic next.

LOWER CUSTOMER LOYALTY

A third area in which the declining legitimacy of banks manifests itself has to do with customer loyalty. Banks have traditionally enshrined customer loyalty and loyalty to their customers among their key business principles. Loyal customers tend to be more profitable, thanks to the bank's ability to cross-sell them more products. A long and strong relationship is also a source of mutual trust. If the banking market is oligopolistic, that is, there are a few large banks that dominate the landscape, losing a customer reduces efficiency because acquiring a replacement customer can be very expensive. These reasons for seeking to increase and maintain customer loyalty are true for both individual and small business customers.

After decades of relatively high and stable levels of customer loyalty in most banking markets, the majority of banks are currently reporting higher rates of customer turnover. This trend is affecting banks in both developed and emerging markets. Surveys show that in some of them as many as 10 or even 20 percent of customers are seriously considering shifting their business to another bank.[3] Needless to say, no bank would be able to operate with such a high rate of customer turnover. But even if the rate is as low as 3 or 5 percent, the bank's efficiency ratio and reputation will suffer massively.

Customers leave a bank for a variety of reasons. Most of the time they choose another bank that offers lower fees, more attractive interest rates, or better service. The true devil, however, is in the details. Turnover rates turn out to be higher among certain types of customers. Younger customers are less loyal to banks in general as well as to any specific bank. This is for three reasons. First, they tend to buy less of an array of products and services than older customers, which reduces switching costs in the form of the hassle involved in moving accounts, loans, and payments to another institution. Second, younger customers are more price sensitive, and are more likely to shop around for better deals. And third, younger customers see more value in new technology-based ways of interacting with the bank, which exacerbates mobility and price comparison. Luckily for banks, acquiring a new customer over the Internet or a mobile banking application is up to half as expensive as doing so through a physical branch, which helps to mitigate the negative impact of turnover among younger customers.

Banks have traditionally sought to increase customer loyalty through means such as:

- **Increasing switching costs.** This is mainly accomplished by cross-selling as many products as possible and providing low-cost or free services that make switching a hassle (e.g., automatic debits for paying bills).

- **Lowering or eliminating fees for customers who agree to certain conditions** such as maintaining minimum balances, directly depositing their salary into their account, and keeping within a set limit of transactions that they can perform.

- **Making special offers to existing customers.**

- **Providing gifts or other rewards for customers who agree to buy certain products and services** like term deposit accounts, pension funds, and insurance.

While effective in the past, many of these tactics may not be as useful to banks in the future. Customers, especially younger ones, are increasingly wary of arrangements that reduce their options or tie them to a specific service provider. Enhanced competition is driving down fees and commissions in many markets. New technology is rapidly reducing switching costs and enabling customers to shop around. Most importantly, technology makes it easy and convenient to buy products and services from different banks or financial providers, and to consolidate all of the relationships in a way that information transfers and payments can be made seamlessly. A savvy customer can nowadays secure a mortgage from a bank, a credit card from an airline company, a mutual fund from a financial services firm, a life insurance policy from a broker, and an automobile loan from a consumer finance company, and she can pay all of her bills or move money around using a mobile app. Although there may ultimately be a bank behind each of these products or services, there is no guarantee or requirement that it will be the same bank. The old value proposition of having a relationship with a single bank is breaking down.

In the face of these challenges, banks have options at their disposal:

- **Multi-brand strategies.** Banks have very rarely ventured down the road of creating or acquiring different brands for different products, services, and segments of the market. Other companies, especially those in consumer nondurables, have refined the art of blanketing the market with different brand offerings that target geographies, sociodemographic segments, price points, and many other relevant variables. This option means that the traditional concept of loyalty is redefined. The goal is to no longer encourage the customer to be loyal to a specific brand for all of her financial needs. Rather, the bank aims to ensure that brand choice is exercised within the array of corporate offerings.

- **Strategic alliances.** Banks around the world have increased their use of strategic alliances with other types of companies in order to reach more customers and offer them more products. This is especially the case with utilities, airlines, and other similar companies with a large customer base. Banks must also tap into the social networks created by large nonprofit organizations, including voluntary associations, charities, churches, and universities.

- **Mergers and acquisitions.** Banks can grow into the rapidly expanding universe of integrated financial services by acquiring assets or businesses, not necessarily entire companies. Some banks have stepped up their efforts to have a presence in new forms of consumer finance, especially in the automobile field. After making some big mistakes during the Internet, new-economy boom at the turn of the twenty-first century, banks have shied away from buying Internet, virtual, or mobile companies, assets, or businesses. They must overcome this inertia and become active participants in the growth and transformation of the technology industry in the same way that venture capital and private equity firms have.

- **New technology.** Surveys show that convenience is the number-one factor when it comes to customer loyalty. In addition, mobile-only bank customers are among the most loyal, in spite of the fact that they have easier ways of switching banks.[4]

- **The concept of the Everyday Bank.** It is important for banks to position themselves as providers of solutions for the customer's everyday life needs and problems. Banks can become the key players in an e-commerce ecosystem on the basis of the relationship with their customers and leveraging the information they possess about them, as we analyze in the next section and in chapter 5.

Customer loyalty in small business banking is driven more by the value of the relationship to the customer than is the case with individuals. As a result, there is not so much erosion in loyalty. Still, it is not clear to what extent new technology may alter the traditional equation. Small businesses are cost conscious, but changing banking relationships too frequently can be highly disruptive, even if cloud computing and the proliferation of apps for all sorts of purposes continue to increase. Thus, we recommend that banks:

- Monitor very closely trends in banking to small business customers in anticipation of potential shifts in loyalty rates above and beyond normal turnover.

- Study the ways in which new technology, especially mobile apps, can enhance the banking relationship and promote loyalty.

- In emerging markets, pursue ways in which new technology may help persuade more individuals and small business owners to become bank customers.

- Unlike for individual customers, offer integrated and single-branded products and services that add value without reducing options.

- Explore alliances and joint ventures that can enable the bank to reach customers in new contexts and create new experiences. This could mean partnering with consumer or digital brands in developed markets to build on positive brand associations, or creating alliances with retailers and telecommunications companies in emerging markets to serve customers beyond the reach of existing banking infrastructure.

EXPANDING THE SCOPE OF WHAT BANKS DO

The idea of the Everyday Bank is one with the potential of not only generating additional revenue streams but also rebuilding the relationship with customers in a way that is value and reputation enhancing. Many customers perceive banks as making money off them whenever they need to move money or borrow money. Most people feel financially constrained and at times financially stressed. Banks could turn these needs into opportunities for a new type of banking, one that both prevents and resolves financial difficulties for customers. Under this model, banks would be more engaged in financial education, providing customers with improved tools and more advisory services before financial needs degenerate into financial problems. Banks would thus become companies that help people better manage their finances through services and analytics, and by facilitating self-learning and peer-to-peer advice.

The crucial element in banks' struggle to regain legitimacy is to become a partner for the customer with a view to improving the economic aspects of his or her life. A large and growing percentage of the public thinks that banks are money-making machines impermeable to customers' wants and needs. In the same way that Apple Inc., made people love computers and smartphones, making them fun and easy to use, banks need to help people view financial services as a life-enhancing experience. Banks need to become providers of solutions. We will explore in chapter 5 how technology can help banks move in this direction.

WINNING THE LEGITIMACY BATTLE

Banks that fail to address their current legitimacy problems will find themselves at a disadvantage in the ever more competitive financial services landscape of the twenty-first century. Legitimacy and trust with customers, regulators, investors, and the general public must be regained and then sustained over time. The consequences of not doing so would be business lost to bank and nonbank competitors, more stringent regulation, and continuing public relations problems. Given the other formidable challenges they are facing—population aging, the skepticism of the millennial generation, nonbank competition, disintermediation, and so on—banks can ill afford to ignore the legitimacy crisis.

CHAPTER 5

Banking and the Digital Transformation

The digital revolution has the potential of transforming every aspect of daily life, and it will most likely lead to a large-scale shake-out in the banking sector. The bank of the future may well be an information-processing company. Telecommunication and information technologies are already changing the ways in which banks relate to their customers and to regulators. Banks are also experimenting with new ways of organizing work internally and networking with other financial and nonfinancial institutions. Big data, for its part, could become the dominant way of analyzing customer profiles and assessing risks, thus relegating relationship-based banking to the background. After all, banks are in possession of vast amounts of information on their customers. As Juan Pedro Moreno of Accenture argued in a recent op-ed piece in the *Financial Times*, "instead of just enabling customers to pay for something, [banks] can move further into their commercial lives by helping them reach the decisions on what to buy, when, and where."[1]

Information technologies pose a threat to the traditional model of relationship-based and branch-centered banking. Over the last half century, banks have successfully incorporated new technologies such as ATMs and computers for data processing and storage. These types of technologies have actually reinforced a business model that places the traditional bank at the center of the financial services industry and the physical branch as the fundamental node in the distribution network, especially when it comes to sales. It is also a model that involves high fixed costs and the associated need for scale.

Banks have always had an ambivalent attitude toward new technology. On the one hand, it helps them reduce costs, reorganize their back-office operations in more efficient ways, and attract technology-savvy customers. On the other, new technology is seen as potentially upsetting the competitive equilibrium among entrenched banks. New technology also has the potential of reducing barriers of entry, thus promoting more competition either by new bank entrants or by disintermediation from nonbank companies. It is worth remembering the extent to which the airline industry was transformed in the late 1990s by the Internet, which allowed consumers to compare prices and make purchases, bypassing traditional distribution channels. Fully taking advantage of the digital revolution will require banks to change their culture as well as significant aspects of their business model.

THE CHALLENGE OF MOBILITY AND CONNECTIVITY

Among the different technologies disrupting competition in a variety of industries, mobile telecommunications and the rise of the mobile web will perhaps have the most impact on banks. There are several reasons for this. The first is that the mobile phone is the first device to be used by nearly the entire population, both in rich and in developing countries (see Figure 5-1). The fixed-line telephone, the personal computer, and the automobile, for instance, did not diffuse as quickly or to as many people. With more than six billion mobile phones in operation, one-third of them smartphones, and the mobile web now surpassing the fixed web in terms of use, mobile telecommunications represents a universe of opportunity. Mobile information processing is likely to become even more revolutionary in the near future as

Figure 5-1. Mobile Phones Per 100 Population

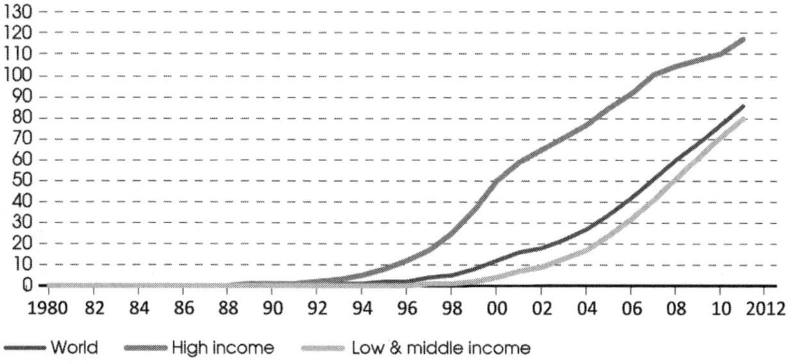

Source: World Development Indicators

wearable computing takes off with devices such as smartwatches and smart eyewear.

The second peculiarity about the mobile phone is that it is exceedingly cheap and easy to use. Telecom companies have managed to turn the phone into a necessity by offering a wide array of services at a relatively affordable price. Moreover, phones are personal devices with low rates of shared consumption (except in poor countries).

The mobile phone is also a device that young people find especially attractive. They relate to their mobile phone in ways that they do not with any other consumer product. The smartphone has become much more than a personal consumption item. It has become a symbol of one's identity, a device that conveys the owner's aspirations.

Finally, the mobile phone is an augmentative device, a pal, and a relationship-enhancing device. The smartphone, in particular, has made virtual social connectivity possible on a scale and with a scope unthinkable just a few years ago. Banks have traditionally dealt with customers one at a time. Digital social media, however, are all about peer comparison and peer consumption. Social networks have become much more important than in the past when it comes to searching, sorting, and prioritizing information regarding purchasing and financial decisions.

Research by Accenture shows that banks prioritize areas of new technology that they can control, such as cloud computing and big data. While they believe facility with mobile technology is a priority, they tend to attach less importance to areas that require more interaction with the customer, such as social media.[2]

Levels of usage of mobile phones for banking services is very heterogeneous around the world. Intriguingly, emerging and even some developing economies are ahead of the pack in terms of mobile banking applications. According to the Aite Group, LLC, more than two-thirds of the adult population of China and India use the mobile phone for checking their account balances or moving money. In the United States and Europe, the percentage is below 40.[3] In Kenya, there are ten times more mobile payments users than bank customers. By the end of 2012, there were nearly thirty countries in Africa, Asia, and Latin America in which the mobile banking infrastructure was greater than the traditional banking infrastructure.[4] Tellingly, most consumers in emerging markets expect the mobile revolution to grow in importance over the next few years, while those in Europe and the United States do not believe it will become an important way of banking. More than three times as many consumers in emerging economies use social networking applications to find out more about financial services, to access their accounts, to share information and offers, and to comment on the level of service received, when compared with consumers in Europe or the United States.[5] Research indicates that people aren't avoiding mobile banking applications because they do not know how to use them; rather, they do not feel they need to, they do not trust them, or their bank does not offer one.

Will mobile payments and mobile banking displace traditional distribution channels and ways of doing banking? What should banks do in the wake of the most important technological discontinuity in nearly a century? Banks would be wise to consider the implications of the information technology revolution as it relates to other important trends affecting financial services:

• Mobile banking is growing faster in emerging and developing countries, precisely the same markets that are expected to monopolize overall growth in financial services over the next decades.

- The young generation of consumers has not yet become bank customers, but they have already become mobile phone users. According to comScore, in the United States 59 percent of mobile banking users are below the age of thirty-five, meaning that mobile banking is the easiest way of attracting and retaining young bank customers.[6]

- Mobile banking may enable new nonbank competitors to enter the market, thus expanding the relevant set of competitors beyond the financial services industry itself. In particular, telecommunication companies have entered the mobile payments sector in many markets, establishing an important beachhead for future expansion into other areas of financial services.

- Mobile phones do not necessarily render physical branches obsolete, but they do require banks to rethink their entire distribution strategy.

WHAT DO BANK CUSTOMERS REALLY WANT?

An important mistake banks could make in response to the mobile revolution is to assume that customers merely want a new distribution channel added to the mix. The mobile revolution is much more than that. A 2013 survey conducted by First Data in ten emerging and developed markets revealed that customers see mobile banking not as a transaction-enabling tool but as an experience that gives them convenience, access to information and new offers, and the ability to get the best possible deal. Most importantly, customers value seamlessness, that is, the ability to move back and forth between the real and the virtual world and across online, mobile, and brick-and-mortar platforms. The survey also found that customers want to be loyal only to the extent that they are rewarded for not switching to another bank.[7]

Banks need to realize that the mobile phone is a device that is radically individualizing and radically social at the same time. Customers want banks to take into consideration their specific circumstances when offering products and services, and they believe that the mobile phone is a tool that should enable any company, including banks, to give them exactly what they want, anytime and anywhere. Customers, however, also want to make purchase decisions in a social way, preferably using their phones. Thus, banks need to find a formula that exploits these two characteristics of this new technology platform.

Banks that successfully embrace the new technology, paying attention to its full potential, stand to benefit handsomely from it. A 2013 Gallup, Inc. poll in the United States found higher conversion rates when banks interacted with potential customers using digital social media. When considering a new financial product, more than half of customers did some research about it. Customers who did research are more likely to make a purchase. But the conversion rate differed massively depending on where the research was done. Customers who did their research through social networks were 18 percent more likely to make a purchase, compared with 9 percent for the bank's website, 8 percent over the phone, and 6 percent at the branch. Still, the poll found that printed material generated a 17 percent lift in conversion, when compared with social networking, which suggests that bank ATMs should be outfitted to allow customers to print brochures with new offers.[8]

Bank customers would like more opportunities for peer-to-peer connectivity and exchange. More and more customers post reviews online, and in some countries, including China and India, nearly 80 percent of online users go to social networks before making a purchase. Banks can no longer ignore the social nature of mobile phones.

MOBILE BANKING: GROWING IN EMERGING MARKETS

Mobile digital media holds great promise in emerging markets precisely because traditional branch-based banking and the payments infrastructure never reached the level of development and saturation that they did in Europe and North America. The statistics are most telling. Whereas more than 80 percent of the adult population in North America and more than 90 percent in Western Europe has at least one account with a formal financial institution, in Latin America the proportion drops to between 15 and 80 percent, and in many African, Middle Eastern, and South Asian countries it can be lower than 5 percent. In China, two-thirds of the adult population has a bank account, while in India it is only one-third.[9]

There are two key aspects of banking markets in emerging economies. The first is that most of their growth will come from new customers who have become middle-class consumers. The second is that technology will play a key role.

The staggering rise of the global middle class has major implications for financial services as well. The middle class is the best customer for commercial banks. Middle-class consumers need loans for buying homes, cars, and appliances; they like to save; they need to move money; and they need insurance products. The fact that these opportunities for growth exist, however, does not mean that banks will automatically become the providers of the services demanded by new middle-class consumers in emerging markets. Depending on tradition and regulation, other types of financial intermediaries may prove faster and more adept at meeting their needs.

Another important feature of middle-class consumption to keep in mind is that it is eminently aspirational. The middle-class consumer purchases goods and services that reflect his new status in society. This means that purchase decisions are not necessarily driven by price but rather by product differentiation. Thus, financial institutions need to convey to the middle-class consumer a sense of distinction and of status.

Mobile phone and/or Internet-based service providers stand to benefit from the rise of the global middle class for several reasons:

• Traditional bank branch networks are underdeveloped in emerging markets.

• Rapid urbanization and the absence of an extensive branch network means that middle-class consumers in emerging markets will value convenience.

• Levels of mobile phone use for financial services are already much higher in emerging markets than in developed markets, in part because the population is much younger and more willing to adopt new digital technologies.

• Regulatory frameworks tend to be less restrictive in some emerging markets than in advanced economies, though they can be more intricate and limiting in others. It is easier for nonbank companies to provide banking services in some emerging economies with less restrictive regulations, and the lack of a physical infrastructure for banking also facilitates the growth of mobile solutions.

It has become readily apparent that only banks with a comprehensive mobile banking strategy will benefit from the growth of financial services in emerging markets, and that banks will not be the only players to benefit from such growth.

TURNING THE YOUNGER GENERATION INTO BANK CUSTOMERS

Banks face a mounting challenge when it comes to persuading young people to become bank customers. Over the next two decades, more than half of the growth in financial services around the world will come from people under the age of thirty. Much of this growth will take place in emerging markets, but a significant proportion will occur in developed markets. Banks risk losing ground relative to other kinds of financial intermediaries.

In developed markets, confidence in banks has plummeted in the wake of the financial crisis, and this has especially affected young people. There are many reasons for this. Young people tend to be more critical of established institutions, and they are more radical in their thinking about the changes needed to address economic, political, and social challenges.

As consumers, young people are different:

• They place more value on the flexibility and convenience of a "bank" that is available everywhere 24/7. This is why the mobile revolution will make such a difference among young bank customers.

• They have become accustomed to using Internet-based content and services for free. This means that they are more reluctant than the average consumer to accept fees and commissions.

• They are more likely to value freedom of choice and are less loyal to a particular service provider.

• They are more brand conscious.

• They are driven by peer approval and sensory brand images to a greater extent.

• However, in many markets they still value the opportunity for face-to-face communication; given that young customers are embarking on their first important financial decisions, it is not surprising that many still value in-person advice.

Young consumers in emerging markets display a more complex behavioral pattern that lies at the intersection of three distinct developments: their newly acquired middle-class status, their technological savvy, and their age. In the near future, most of the growth in global financial services will take place among this demographic in emerging markets.

Banks must consider different ways of addressing this challenge in order to secure their future as the most important financial intermediaries in emerging markets, and to prevent young consumers in developed markets from defecting to other types of intermediaries. Among the ways they might address this are:

- Establishing a long-term relationship with young customers
- Abolishing fees and commissions in favor of membership charges that bundle a variety of services in exchange for convenience, product differentiation, security, and advice.
- Fully integrating the physical and virtual ways of bank-customer interaction

MOBILE BANKING FOR SMALL BUSINESSES

The impact of the mobile banking revolution will be different in the case of small business customers. For starters, small businesses are more willing to pay for mobile banking services than individual customers.[10] Moreover, mobile banking offers small businesses many ways of cutting costs and enhancing value for their own customers, especially in the areas of mobile payments and mobile short-term loans.

Research indicates that small businesses are more inclined to value a close, trusting relationship with the bank than are individual customers, who tend to be motivated to a greater extent by price. Mobile banking, with its potential for building on and generating networks of relationships, holds great promise for banking small businesses.

Digital technology can potentially expand the range of services that banks offer to small businesses. Banks can provide small firms with integrated billing and administration solutions, payment collection services, and even e-commerce platforms so they can reach new markets and new customers.

The future of mobile banking for small business is especially promising in emerging markets. There are many micro, small, and medium enterprises that are currently unserved or underserved by banks: 25 million in Latin America, 30 million in sub-Saharan Africa, 41 million in South Asia, and 125 million in East Asia, mostly China, Vietnam, and the Philippines.[11] As is the case with individual customers, given the lack of a brick-and-mortar network of bank branches, mobile banking is the ideal technology to turn these companies into bank customers.

In advanced markets, mobile banking may also induce cash-based small businesses to change their views about electronic payments, as long as they are offered convenience, security, and flexibility. Square, for instance, has persuaded more than four million merchants to accept its new form of payment, and approximately 60 percent of them did not previously accept credit or debit cards. This example shows that new technology can be used to expand the boundaries of financial services to include new customers.

THE THREAT OF NEW COMPETITORS

The banking sector has become much more porous than in the past, in the sense that it is easier for competitors to enter the industry. New forms of doing finance and new technology have altered the landscape. Nonbank competitors have entered the banking landscape quickly and in ways that have started to put even the most entrenched banks on the defensive:

- **Payment systems.** The growth of PayPal, Dwolla, iBeacon™, iZettle, and similar payments companies has taken the banking sector by storm. Adding to this threat, companies such as Google, Walmart, and Starbucks Corporation, have entered the space with great celerity and backed up by the corporations' huge financial muscle.

- **Electronic marketplaces.** These have grown very quickly, especially those catering to the needs of small businesses seeking to offer their unpaid invoices to investors at a discount.

- **Big suppliers to small businesses** such as Amazon.com, Inc., Kabbage, Inc., or Alibaba.com Hong Kong Limited offer credit as an integral part of their service.

- **Peer-to-peer platforms.** Consumers and small firms loan to each other using an electronic marketplace.

- **Storefront operators.** Here the typical arrangement is a virtual company that offers full-service banking from a smartphone, handling FDIC-insured deposits through an agreement with a conventional bank.

- **Mobile telecommunications companies.** These include companies from M-Pesa™ in Kenya to ISSI, Inc., and T-Mobile US Inc., Mobile Money™ in the U.S.

- **Disintermediators** like Square and Moven, which provide a customer management layer between the customer and the banking utility, creating a better user experience.

- **Bitcoin and other alternative currencies** creating new value stores and forms of exchange outside traditional banking and payment systems.

Some observers argue that these nonbank competitors have gained the upper hand because they remain unregulated. Once they are forced to play under the same rules as conventional banks, the thinking goes, their advantages will disappear. This logic is flawed for two fundamental reasons. First, some banking authorities have begun to regulate electronic marketplaces, as in Britain. Second, regulation may actually help them grow faster because it will help them establish trust and legitimacy.

INCREMENTAL OR RADICAL?

Many banks react to new technological breakthroughs by adding new features, options, or channels. Often, they create separate departments or units to run the new systems in parallel with existing ones. For instance, many banks continue to run their physical branch networks and their virtual operations separately. In some cases customers need to dial a different number to get assistance regarding physical versus virtual transactions.

Research shows that it is generally a mistake to incorporate mobile banking innovations in a piecemeal fashion for the mass market.[12] Some of the problems a bank may encounter when innovating incrementally in the digital world include:

• New channel availability will likely increase the number of transactions without necessarily generating revenue and profits for the bank.

• Customers may experience differences in price and quality of service across channels, with the corresponding negative effects on customer satisfaction and loyalty.

• Banks may lose opportunities for cross-selling if some products and services are offered only through certain channels.

• Banks may suffer in terms of reputation and brand image as customers using different channels have different experiences.

• As customers move towards direct channels, their interactions tend to be more transactional and less sticky. Providers of mobile financial services will need to create richer experiences in direct channels to maintain relationship engagement.

Banks would be wise to think carefully about how to deploy new technology, especially mobile banking applications. There are two key decisions that they need to make. The first has to do with the virtues of incremental versus radical innovations, and the second regards the target segment, that is, the mass market of its entire customer base or a specific niche or demographic. We believe that

Figure 5-2. Examples of Different Kinds of Mobile Banking Innovations

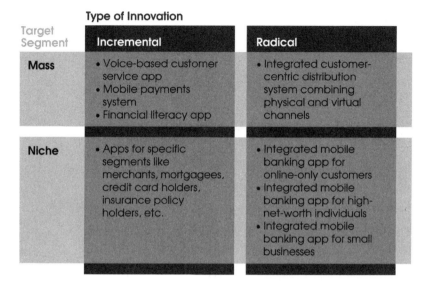

Target Segment	Type of Innovation	
	Incremental	**Radical**
Mass	• Voice-based customer service app • Mobile payments system • Financial literacy app	• Integrated customer-centric distribution system combining physical and virtual channels
Niche	• Apps for specific segments like merchants, mortgagees, credit card holders, insurance policy holders, etc.	• Integrated mobile banking app for online-only customers • Integrated mobile banking app for high-net-worth individuals • Integrated mobile banking app for small businesses

there are sound reasons for a bank to pursue different combinations of incremental and radical innovations in mobile banking for both the mass market and for niche segments.

Figure 5-2 shows a few relevant examples. Banks may pursue incremental innovations for the mass market such as voice-based customer service apps, mobile payments systems, and financial literacy apps. We would emphasize the importance of eliminating incentives for customers to increase the number of transactions without generating some revenue and profit for the bank. In addition, banks should be watchful not to lose any cross-selling opportunities due to a lack of coordination between these incremental innovations and other existing channels.

Banks may also pursue incremental mobile innovations for niche segments such as merchants, mortgagees, credit card holders, insurance policy holders, and so on. The danger here is in fragmenting the bank's customer base into compartmentalized groups without seeing the opportunities for cross-selling. The ostensible advantage involves designing and tailoring the apps to the specific needs of those segments or customer groups. We would urge caution in pursuing this type of strategy.

Given the growing importance of emerging economies with underbranched banking markets, and the characteristics of the millennial generation, we believe that the big opportunities in mobile banking involve radical innovations. By radical innovation we mean a set of actions that transform the ways in which the bank does business with its customers. For niche segments, banks may think about integrated mobile banking apps for specific customer groups such as high-net-worth individuals or small businesses. We would caution about segmenting the bank's customer base solely in terms of online-only and traditional customers. Rather, banks will need to mine customer data to find behavioral patterns. For the mass market, one option is to pursue a strategy of an integrated customer-centric distribution system combining physical and virtual channels. Below, we explain what the prerequisites and the implications of this approach are.

REINVENTING THE BANK BRANCH

For many large commercial banks, the physical branch network typically represents up to 50 percent of the overall cost base. As more customers use mobile channels, banks need to revisit their cost structure. Branches, however, are still vital, as a branding magnet as well as to nurture and support the most important sales relationships. One key principle is to refocus branches away from manual transactions and toward the most important (and often profitable) activities of relationship-based banking and advisory services. This means more technology in the branch for self- and assisted service.

Radical innovation with mobile banking applications necessarily requires a new approach to the way in which the bank reaches customers and does business with them. The most important manifestation of the presence of a bank in the market is the physical branch. Over the last few decades, bank branches have evolved to occupy the center stage of the bank's strategy and organization. Bank branches play a crucial role as:

- A hub in which the customer can access all of the services offered by the bank.
- A magnet that enables the bank to offer additional services to existing customers when they visit the branch.
- A barrier to entry to the extent that an extensive branch network by incumbent banks makes it hard for new entrants to gain a foothold in the market.
- The basic organizational cell in the bank's overall architecture, given that many departments, positions, and tasks are allocated across branches, and that many measures of profitability are broken all the way down to the branch level.

Much of what banks need to do in order to successfully incorporate new mobile technology involves rethinking and restructuring their branch networks. Banks, however, can make two mistakes in attempting to reconfigure their brick-and-mortar operations to accommodate mobile banking. The first would be to think that new technology will eventually make physical branches irrelevant, and the second would be to believe that their branch strategy does not need to change in the wake of the mobile technology revolution. Branches are here to stay, but they must be differentiated in terms of location, format, and function:

- **Flagship branches.** Branches in the mold of Apple Stores® retail store services generate hype, attract new customers, and generate brand awareness. Although expensive, they can play a key role when it comes to bringing new services to the market. Flagship branches focus on enhancing loyalty and generating sales, not on transactions.
- **Full-service neighborhood and workplace branches.** This is the type of branch that comes closest to the traditional.

The hub branch, however, needs to be more open, participatory, and attractive, especially from the point of view of young customers. The branch should be totally integrated with mobile and online channels so that the customer can initiate the transaction before arriving at the branch, and therefore reduce or eliminate waiting times. Full-service branches would both generate sales and enable transactions. At the same time, neighborhood branches need to continue offering a place in which small businesses can interact with the bank and obtain the full range of services that they need in order to operate.

- **Kiosks at high-traffic locations.** These outlets could have one or two employees, and allow customers to perform quick transactions that require human intervention. They may also provide customers with advice on specific issues. Kiosks would focus on transactions rather than sales.

- **Smart ATMs.** Conventional ATM technology is more than four decades old. A smart ATM receives and dispenses cash in any combination of bills and coins, checks, stamps, shipping labels, prepaid cards, prepaid tickets, boarding passes, and so on. The idea here is not to charge the customer a fee for these services, but rather to help the customer who wants to spend as little time running errands as possible. It is also important to enable the customer to print brochures with new product offerings, given the high conversion rate that this medium of interaction ensures.[13] Smart ATMs would focus on transactions and on convenience.

- **Touch-screen walls in waiting areas.** These are for customers to learn about financial services, products, and more broadly about finance and other topics, rather than to perform transactions. Interactive workspaces and assisted advisory technology—where bank agents and customers can work together—efficiently capture customer data and requirements.

It is important to highlight that each of these types of branches will need to be integrated for branding consistency and in order to ensure that the customer can move seamlessly across channels.

MOBILE BANKING STRATEGIES THAT WORK

It is important for banks to think about mobile banking as a progression of different stages.[14] As banks acquire experience with mobile banking, they can incorporate more features and be more comprehensive about their approach. Case studies of banks in both advanced and emerging economies indicate that banks need to design a credible strategy for persuading a large number of customers to use mobile banking. Otherwise, the return on investment will suffer. The four main stages in the implementation of mobile banking are as follows:

• **Informational:** Many banks have started their mobile banking strategy by using the channel to relay information to their existing customers, including balances, transaction history, SMS alerts, ATM finders, credit or debit card fraud detection, etc.

• **Transactional:** A second stage in mobile banking focuses on transactions such as remote deposit capture, balance transfers, bill paying, stock trading, and peer-to-peer (P2P) payments.

• **Interactive:** It is only in a third stage that the bank starts to fully utilize the innovative features of mobile telecommunications, extending its services to actionable alerts, personal financial management, mass marketing, and transaction verification.

• **Orchestrative:** The full-blown mobile banking model would include location- and context-specific offers and prompts, lifestyle management, cross-channel process management, and opt-in preferences. Some banks like Commonwealth Bank of Australia (CBA) Hana Bank, mBank, and Garanti have made great inroads in terms of implementing an orchestrative approach to mobile banking.

In order to drive up usage rates, experience shows that fees need to be minimal, customer education is key, attractive rewards may have to be used, and spam-like contact with customers must be minimal. The mobile phone is perceived as an intimate, private device, and thus banks must be cautious about both situational cross-selling and generic offers.[15] Customers see their phone as a liberating device, meaning that banks ought to let customers bundle the products and services they would like to use. This kind of dynamic bundling can become an effective tool for cross-selling to existing customers and for attracting new customers.[16] The main challenges are always to provide convenience and service combined with security and privacy.[17]

The mobile banking model represents a very different way of banking than the way in which most banks interact with customers today. In its *Banking 2016* report, Accenture proposed that the bank of the future should be:

- **Multichannel:** with an integrated and dynamic architecture
- **Intelligent:** including real-time, need-based offerings of products
- **Socially engaging:** focused on relationship-based banking
- **Beyond financial services:** serving as a lifestyle supermarket
- **Ubiquitous:** embracing mobility in all of its aspects

Increasingly, banks are incorporating several of these features in novel and creative ways. The challenge facing banks is how to make it profitable to deliver such a complex, and radically new, approach to financial services to individual customers and small businesses. Mobile technology has to make money for the bank as well as add value to the customer, but it cannot be in the form of fees and commissions. Rather, banks should incorporate new technology so that they can obtain two main benefits:

- **Customer loyalty.** The cost of acquiring a new customer has grown, especially if it involves stealing the customer away from a competitor. Banks cannot afford to lose existing or potential customers for lack of attention to new technology. This is particularly the case with young customers.

- **Additional income through product and service bundling.** Banks should generate profits from mobile banking by bundling financial services with an array of mobile commerce. Given that attack is the best form of defense, banks should take the initiative and invade other sectors by turning themselves into service hubs, or lifestyle supermarkets, in which they offer their customers the ability to access leisure, entertainment, shopping, and other services as well as financial products. This strategy may be especially effective with durable goods such as automobiles, appliances, and furniture due to the customer's desire for information before making a purchase and because of the associated demand for credit.

Research undertaken by Accenture shows that mobile technology has the potential to reverse banks' falling reputation, enhance customer experience, and be profitable, as long as internal processes are integrated. Without process realignment, the promise of mobile banking is unlikely to be realized, and returns on investment in new technologies could be low or even negative.[18]

Without a doubt, mobile technology is poised to play an increasingly important role in the overall strategy of companies in most industries. In the banking sector radical innovation will necessarily mean a rethinking of the way most people have traditionally interacted with financial institutions. Demographic, regulatory, and economic trends are putting pressure on banks to become more innovative. Mobile banking, done properly, can become a way for banks to successfully adapt to change.

BEYOND MOBILE BANKING: BANKS AS INFORMATION COMPANIES

The new possibilities offered by telecommunication and information technologies extend well beyond distribution channels and the relationship with customers. Banks have an opportunity to become much more than just money and risk managers. They can become information hubs for the digital economy and e-commerce. Banks have more information about their individual and small business customers than any other type of firm, including data about their income, savings, expenses, and investment patterns. Turning themselves into information companies would create new opportunities for banks:

• Banks could move beyond the bundling of financial services to position themselves at the center of an e-commerce ecosystem in which they not only facilitate payments and provide credit but also sell information and offer deals about a full range of products and services offered by other companies. In many ways, this would turn banks into online intermediaries like Amazon.com or Alibaba.com, but armed with the ability to operate as financial intermediaries as well as information brokers.

• A bank positioned at the center of the e-commerce ecosystem would be in a unique position to offer credit and other financial products to both sides of the transaction, i.e., sellers and buyers.

• Banks may also develop other parts of the financial and e-commerce infrastructure by providing ratings of both sellers and buyers, and by shaping supply and demand through special offers and deals.

• Finally, banks focused on e-commerce would be better positioned to offer customers the kind of end-to-end solutions they long for. For instance, the bank could create an e-commerce platform that helps buyers look for advice on which automobile to buy, where to get the best deal, what loan to obtain, which insurance product to buy, and whether a repair-and-parts plan makes sense or not.

It is important to note that banks need not develop a full-blown e-commerce platform extending across many categories of goods and services from the beginning. As the example about automobiles illustrates, banks can launch specialized e-commerce platforms in those specific areas in which they feel they have the knowledge and the capabilities to do so. They can also target those areas in which they wish to grow. Having said that, there are a number of network effects and tipping-point dynamics that banks will need to study carefully in order to choose which e-commerce ecosystems to create. The guiding principles when selecting the ways in which to turn themselves into information companies should be:

- Is the strategy conducive to enhanced customer satisfaction and retention?
- Are there synergies between the bank's financial activity and the proposed e-commerce platform?
- Does the bank possess proprietary information about customers that no other firm has access to, and thus represents a source of sustainable competitive advantage?

The digital transformation of the banking business is proceeding very rapidly. At a minimum, banks must change the way in which they relate to customers, especially taking into account the mobile revolution and the desire of the younger generation for technology-mediated interaction. In emerging markets, technology-savvy banks are likely to grow faster than those that do not embrace it. In addition, the digital telecommunication and information revolution creates new opportunities for banks to become the key player at the center of e-commerce ecosystems.

CHAPTER 6

Operating in a New Landscape

The banking industry is facing unprecedented changes in its competitive landscape. Banks will have to completely adapt their business models to survive in an environment where failures and exits are not going to be as exceptional as they used to be. The sequels of the worst financial crisis in eight decades will have extremely important implications for the competitive structure of the banking sector, for customer trust (anger, frustration, decline in loyalty), and for the behavior of banking authorities (regulatory, fiscal, etc.). But it would be unwise to consider the crisis and its sequels as the only factors shaping the future of the banking industry, as we have argued in the preceding chapters.

Macro Trends: Economic, Demographic, and Sociological

Banks will need to digest the consequences of the crisis and, at the same time, cope with a series of long-term, structural changes on the demographic, economic, and technological fronts. This combination of forces creates an explosive mix that must be handled with care. For many banks, the business model will need to change in terms of customer attraction and retention, revenue sources, risk management, and growth strategy.

It would be a mistake to think of demographic changes, and particularly population aging, as merely affecting customer relationships and the range of products that need to be offered. This shift will also bring important implications to the banking business in terms of the structure of assets and liabilities, balance-sheet strength, growth strategies, distribution channel mix, and skill requirements for personnel because patterns of savings and borrowing will change. It is also key to realize that population aging is taking place not only in the richest economies but also in some of the largest emerging markets.

The growth of the emerging economies represents a second structural trend that will fundamentally reshape the opportunities for growth. The shift in the center of gravity for middle-class consumption away from Europe and the United States and toward the emerging world—by 2035 two-thirds of the global market will be in the BRICS countries—should create many opportunities for financial services because $30 trillion worth of new middle-class consumption will be created. These markets, however, will not be easy for foreign banks to enter, even by acquisition. Ultimately, the response of banks to the growth of emerging economies will involve difficult trade-offs in terms of the allocation of resources across markets—including both balance-sheet strength and managerial attention. Banks find themselves at a crossroads precisely at a time when their strength and margin for action are substantially reduced as a result of the global financial crisis.

It is also key to consider middle-class consumer behavior in terms of its pronounced brand orientation and the value placed on commitment and loyalty. The central idea here is to offer differentiation on the scale needed to serve the large emerging middle-class markets, that is, a mass-premium strategy emphasizing a certain degree of exclusivity within an affordable price range.

Last but not least, the banking landscape will be deeply disrupted and transformed by the revolution in connectivity and mobility enabled by new technology. For the last half century, banks have made huge investments in technology in order to make their back-office operations more efficient, take advantage of arbitrage opportunities in different markets, and meet customer needs and demands.

However, this time around circumstances seem to be conspiring to erode the traditional business model of banks, and they must consider the potentially disruptive aspects of new technology. Some of the most revolutionary possibilities include a world in which a widely available peer-to-peer platform enables people and small businesses to obtain credit and make deposits, or to secure any other type of financial service, without the intervention of a financial intermediary. Another possibility is a world in which new technology enables nonbank competitors—telecommunications companies, big retailers, and so on—to launch a wide variety of financial products and services. Another potentiality is a world in which banks reinvent themselves and occupy a central position in a transformed financial services industry in which virtual and brick-and-mortar components offer customers a seamless experience.

These scenarios are not mutually exclusive. In fact, the future will not be determined only by technology, but its confluence with demographic, economic, and financial trends will pose distinct challenges for banks. Their business model and strategies have been rendered at least partially obsolete due, in part, to the changes in regulation and competitive dynamics stemming from the global financial crisis.

Regulation

As if the trends and transformations were not enough, banks should expect their margin of maneuver to be much more restricted than in previous decades due to regulation changes. Lax regulation and slack supervision have been widely cited as reasons that the deepest banking crisis in almost a century was not prevented. Authorities have responded by completely overhauling existing banking regulations.

The new regulatory environment tries to eliminate some of the perverse incentives that induced excessive risk taking by banks, as well as the asymmetric distribution of profits and losses in an industry that enjoys safety nets not available to other sectors.

From the point of view of the banks themselves, while regulation acts as a restrictor and reduces managerial degrees of freedom, it should not be seen as a hindrance. It may well create opportunities for banks to differentiate and to rebuild their reputation. Ultimately, tighter regulations may help the better banks stand out from the crowd.

Under the new regulatory scheme, banks will be required to have much more capital of the highest quality. The crisis has demonstrated that the level of capital required prior to 2008 was clearly insufficient to cover losses in adverse scenarios. Better-capitalized banks should be perceived by markets and investors as less risky than in the past, and therefore risk premia and return on equity should be lower, at least on a new steady-state approach. However, the transition period, where banks are required to increase capital while markets have not yet adjusted to the new low-risk environment, opens clear opportunities for better-managed banks to rebuild their capital base sooner and under better conditions than other banks. Regulation therefore creates opportunities for good and nimble banks to surge ahead of competitors.

Large and complex banks will be required to meet capital surcharges to cover the extra systemic risk they represent. This measure tries to counteract the so-called "too big to fail" advantage that large banks enjoy in terms of cheaper financing costs. More importantly, in many countries large and complex banks will be forced to separate commercial banking activities (protected by government guarantees) from other, riskier banking activities on the investment side. These structural reforms aim at ring fencing core from noncore banking activities, and avoid the latter being subsidized by the former.

Consumer protection concerns will be at the core of the new regulatory landscape as a response to some alleged abuses by banks during the crisis, including the mis-selling of financial products, manipulation of prices and indices, and excessive charges in payment operations. These, as well as security and confidentiality concerns (exacerbated by the growth of mobile and Internet banking), will produce a regulatory agenda more friendly to customers. This trend creates clear opportunities for banks to move proactively, faster than new regulations require, and differentiate themselves from competitors.

New taxes will be imposed on banks and other financial firms in several markets around the world as a way to compensate for the negative externalities that they have imposed on society and on public finances. Movements in this direction, however, will have to be coordinated in an international context, as banking activities and financial operations can easily move across countries in search of tax optimization. Banks with superior internal management systems may be able to take advantage of shifting tax regimes, especially if they involve several countries.

Competition

Changes in regulation and taxation will have implications for the competitive structure of banking, already in a state of flux as a result of the crisis, and for corporate mergers and acquisitions.

Excess banking capacity in developed countries contrasts sharply with the large growth potential in most emerging and developing countries. Dealing with this asymmetry is the main challenge and opportunity for large banks with a global strategy. The increasing prospects of mobile banking, and the ease with which customers can switch banks without physical contact, will increase the opportunities to exploit economies of scale and information across national jurisdictions, in order to capture growth opportunities on a global scale.

The presence of the public sector in some banks, as a result of the crisis, creates important challenges and opportunities for the rest of banks. In the short term, state presence may constitute an exit barrier that allows some inefficient banks to keep alive and generate unhealthy competition with consequent pressure on banking margins. In the long term, however, the return of rescued banks to private hands, or even the closing down of some of them, will end up restoring competition and opening growth opportunities for banks showing financial strength and a proven record of excellence in customer service.

Markets assign more value to banks that are better capitalized over others that are less so. This is at odds with complaints usually made against regulatory requirements for higher capitalization levels. Size by itself is not valued by markets, as it is not a guarantee for competitive advantage, and some banks should even think in terms of shedding uncompetitive business lines, as many have already done, especially in Europe and the United States. In fact, pressures to rebuild profitability will lead banks to focus on what they can do best and on what they are in a better competitive position to undertake profitably. Inside each business line, however, there will be ample room for reaping economies of scale, not only in terms of cost savings but especially in terms of information management and customer orientation.

Progress in information technology will increase the availability of "hard" (quantifiable, verifiable) information on borrowers, therefore reducing the advantage that banks have over their customers thanks to "soft" (proprietary) information accumulated through existing bank-customer relationships. Bank customers will then become more contestable, and hard information will make bank operations more scalable.

Pay and recruiting policies in banking will be strongly conditioned by regulatory pressures and by the competitive forces shaping the new banking landscape. An increase in the overall level of regulation, pressures to step back from riskier activities, and a focus on a narrower approach to bank competitiveness will reduce the excess payments that top bank employees have enjoyed during the last three decades relative to other sectors. At the same time, however, there will be a new war for talent in activities more centered on extracting value from big data on customers, as well as exploiting the potential of new technologies in gaining access to a broader segment of clients, in an environment with lower entry and exit barriers. This will lead to more pay discrimination inside banks, as well as more variability in payment levels, linking them to performance on a risk-adjusted basis.

The potential for further growth in the shadow banking system will rest on the relative regulatory burden between the "official" and the "shadow" sides of the industry. Additionally, new forms of direct finance from savers to investors, such as crowdfunding, and peer-to-peer lending, will grow as an alternative to bank-based intermediation, especially for start-ups and SMEs. This is because matching funders with project developers will be more efficient and effective due to the lower search costs involved.

Large data companies from Google to Vodafone will be wondering if they should perform more of the transactional roles of the banking system that are, after all, just data transmission. However, these potential new entrants will need to critically examine which value-adding banking activities to perform, and whether they are prepared to manage issues of liquidity, settlement, risk management, and leverage. Entry of these large data managers into the banking business is one of the greatest threats that traditional banks will face in the new competitive landscape. Such entry will be facilitated not only by the advantages that these companies have in big data management, but also because the banks have lost one of the most important entry barriers that they have enjoyed historically: trust and legitimacy.

Legitimacy

The decline in trust faced by banks worldwide has been compounded by the revelations about the incentives and compensation that were offered to top executives, traders, and other bank personnel, even as their banks went bust or had to be bailed out by taxpayers.

Another area in which the declining legitimacy of banks manifests itself has to do with customer loyalty. The trend toward lower bank customer loyalty is accelerated by the increasing role of technology in banking. New technology is rapidly reducing switching costs, and enabling customers to shop around. This is why some banks may have an ambivalent attitude toward new technology. On the one hand, it helps them reduce costs, reorganize their back-office operations in more efficient ways, and attract technology-savvy customers. On the other hand, new technology has the potential of reducing barriers of entry, thus promoting more competition. While technology has enabled many banks to cut costs and meet customer expectations, it is not clear that it has given banks a sustainable competitive advantage. In many cases, a technology "arms race" has resulted, with few palpable gains.

Application of information technology is also leading banks to question the traditional model of relationship-based and branch-centered banking, a model that involves high fixed costs. Mobile telecommunications and the rise of the mobile web create very different future scenarios for banks. The mobile phone is the first device to be owned by nearly the entire world population; it is both exceedingly cheap and easy to use. The mobile phone is an augmentative device, a gadget that projects one's life and personality toward others.

Mobile digital media holds great promise in emerging markets precisely because the traditional branch-based banking and payments infrastructure never reached the level of development and saturation, as it has done in Europe and North America. Additionally, mobile banking in these developing countries will be the most important way to persuade the young population to become bank customers. Young consumers in emerging markets display a more complex behavioral pattern that lies at the intersection of three distinct developments: their newly acquired middle-class status, their technological savvy, and their age. In the near future, most of the growth in global financial services will take place among this demographic in emerging markets. As customer interactions become more digital, banks will have to combat the trend of customer relationships becoming more transactional and arm's length. Instead they must mature their digital technology investment to create engagement, sustain high-value human touch, and deliver richer interactions mediated through technology.

TOWARD A NEW BUSINESS MODEL

The economic, demographic, technological, competitive, regulatory, and reputational challenges faced by banks at the present time cannot be dealt with in a piecemeal fashion because they are inextricably linked to one another. Adapting to the new financial services landscape will take much more than tinkering with a few elements of the business model, a strategy that banks have successfully deployed during past decades.

Accenture has proposed a methodology for designing and implementing new business models; it has three steps. First, it identifies five main dimensions that companies will need to address, namely, strategic alignment, customer interface, internal processes, human resources and incentives. Second, it links each of these areas to the relevant drivers of change in the industry so it can establish which actions will be required to cope with them and to take advantage of new opportunities. And third, it identifies the key capabilities that companies need to develop in order to successfully adapt and compete in the new landscape.

Banks need to undergo this type of exercise in order to adapt to the complex forces reshaping their competitive landscape. In order to be effective, the process of change toward a new business model must consider the main strategic dimensions and how they interact with the drivers of change identified in the preceding chapters.

Strategic Dimensions

Figure 6-1 lays out the five dimensions for action. Each bank needs to analyze its strategic alignment and how it is supposed to translate this into internal processes and a customer interface that enables the bank to organize its operations. The other two key components are the quantity and quality of human resources required, and the incentives needed to keep the organization focused on the key drivers of profitability.

Strategic Dimensions and the Drivers of Change

The second step is to map how each of the drivers of change identified in the previous chapters affects the five dimensions. We outline in Figure 6-2 what this exercise entails. Each bank must go through

Figure 6-1. Banking Strategic Dimensions to Approach New Business Models

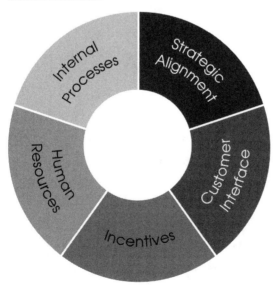

Source: Accenture, May 2014

Figure 6-2. Strategic Dimensions: Interaction with Drivers of Change in the Banking Landscape

Banking Strategic Dimensions \ Drivers of Change	Macro trends				Regulation					Competition						Legitimacy			
	Aging	New young generation	Emerging markets	Global middle class	New capital & liquidity requirements	Separation of activities	Risk management requirements	Consumer protections	New taxes	Excess capacity	Disintermediation & new competitors	New technologies	Customer focus	Talent war	Economies of scale	Lack of trust	Customer loyalty	Stakeholders relationship model	Criticism about incentives & compensation
Strategic alignment	√		√√	√√		√√				√√	√√	√√			√√	√√	√√		
Incentives		√			√√		√√		√√	√		√√				√√		√√	
Human resources			√				√	√					√√	√√			√√		√√
Internal processes		√			√√	√√	√√	√√			√√	√√		√			√√	√	
Customer interface	√√	√√						√√				√√					√√	√√	

Source: Accenture, May 2014

a detailed analysis of the relevant cells in the figure, noting how each of the drivers of change is likely to affect each of its specific businesses. For instance, banking to individuals will be affected differently than banking to small businesses, and wealth management will be impacted in vastly different ways than retail banking. More specifically:

• **Strategic alignment.** Banks should consider how to position themselves in the new banking ecosystem that has emerged out of the crisis and the long-term macro trends. This includes: overall dimension and scope of activities, global allocation of resources, and risk profile. As the broadest scope dimension for the new business model, strategic alignment interacts with virtually all of the drivers of change developed throughout this book.

The interactions are much more intense with macro trends related to the rise of emerging markets and the global middle class, as both of them will clearly alter the global profile of the users of banking services. In the same vein, competitive challenges like excess capacity in developed countries, technological change, and the emergence of new competitors are among the key drivers of change interacting with strategic alignment.

Finally, in terms of regulation and legitimacy, mandatory separation of activities and pressures to restore trust and loyalty, as well as investor confidence, are the most important drivers of change interrelating with strategic alignment.

- **Customer interface.** This dimension includes the value proposition offered to customers and how the relationship with them is going to be defined, both in terms of the substance and the interface. This dimension of the banking business is highly sensitive to changes in demography, especially those related to aging and to the emergence of a new, young generation with a completely new attitude toward financial services.

   Regulatory issues will also be relevant in terms of new and enhanced customer protection. Perhaps the most significant aspects in this part of the analysis, especially when seen in the context of declining trust, should be customer attraction, loyalty, and retention. Start-up innovation, industry convergence, and customer technology adoption will all change expectations for the customer experience delivered by financial providers.

- **Internal processes.** Cost-saving pressures will be a major consideration for banks to deal with in terms of their internal processes. Perhaps the most significant adjustment will come from technological change, both in back-office operations and in supporting the customer interface as processes become increasingly digitalized. Regulatory requirements will translate into changes to internal risk models, capital requirements, and separation of activities, all of them increasing the pressures when designing new internal processes. Interactions with customers will be increasingly mediated by technology, especially mobile technology, and enhanced by data analytics.

• **Human resources.** People and talent will be key in the new banking landscape and model, where highly skilled and motivated personnel will be needed to face apparently contradictory pressures coming from regulation, competition, and new customer needs. Among the drivers of change that interact with the human dimension are those related to customer focus and the need to restore customer loyalty. Extremely important for this dimension are also the challenges posed by compensation policies, which are going to be subject to new regulatory restrictions and transparency requirements. All of this will happen in a setting where talented people need to be attracted to an industry that has lost some of its former appeal.

• **Incentives.** Pressure from public opinion and regulatory authorities are not the only drivers banks should take into consideration when rethinking their incentive systems. Perhaps more important is the need to use incentives tactically to achieve strategic alignment within the new competitive landscape and with shifting demographic, economic, and technological trends. When it comes to regulatory pressures, incentives will need to be overhauled to meet new risk-management guidelines.

Capabilities Analysis

Figure 6-3 summarizes the key capabilities that banks will need to develop in order to successfully adapt and develop their strategic alignment, customer interface, internal processes, human resources, and incentives. When it comes to strategic alignment the key capabilities include the ability to scan the market for new opportunities, flexibility, and adaptability, all of which are required to cope with the main drivers of change in this category, namely, excess capacity, new competitors, disintermediation, new regulations, and changing demographics and markets. Banks should adopt metrics and benchmarks that enable them to track their progress in terms of their ability to anticipate the effects of these changes. Figure 6-3 also includes a simplified list of change drivers (for the complete list, please refer to Figure 6-2).

Adjusting the customer interface to the new realities of the banking landscape in the twenty-first century requires embracing

Figure 6-3. Strategic Dimensions, Drivers of Change, and Key Capabilities

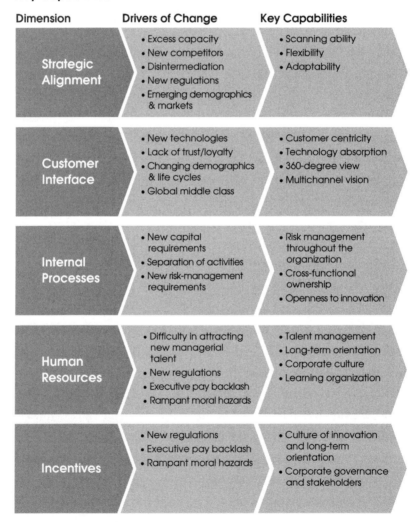

Dimension	Drivers of Change	Key Capabilities
Strategic Alignment	• Excess capacity • New competitors • Disintermediation • New regulations • Emerging demographics & markets	• Scanning ability • Flexibility • Adaptability
Customer Interface	• New technologies • Lack of trust/loyalty • Changing demographics & life cycles • Global middle class	• Customer centricity • Technology absorption • 360-degree view • Multichannel vision
Internal Processes	• New capital requirements • Separation of activities • New risk-management requirements	• Risk management throughout the organization • Cross-functional ownership • Openness to innovation
Human Resources	• Difficulty in attracting new managerial talent • New regulations • Executive pay backlash • Rampant moral hazards	• Talent management • Long-term orientation • Corporate culture • Learning organization
Incentives	• New regulations • Executive pay backlash • Rampant moral hazards	• Culture of innovation and long-term orientation • Corporate governance and stakeholders

Source: Accenture, May 2014

customer centricity as the overarching principle and capability, with technology absorption being the key enabler. Banks will also need to develop the capability to integrate channels into a multichannel vision, and to adopt a 360-degree view of the customer.

Internal processes will need to become more cross-functional and allow for risk management procedures to take place throughout the organization. Most importantly, internal process must adapt to new capital requirements and separation of activities rules without reducing the scope of innovation.

The challenges of building a new human resource system that enables banks to cope with new regulations, moral hazards, and backlash against excessive pay will not be easy to overcome. Talent management capabilities will need to be developed, along with a corporate culture that values customer satisfaction, long-term orientation, and organizational learning and innovation. And, increasingly, banks will need to learn how to harness resources and talent from outside their organizations, including third-party capability providers, alliance partners, and extended workforces.

Finally, incentives need to be overhauled in response to new regulations concerning risk and customer protection, the backlash against excessive compensation, and moral hazards. The key capabilities will be to enhance corporate governance and stakeholder relations, and nurturing an innovative culture focused on the long term. An additional strategic capability will be to adjust to the pace of change in the business landscape, macro trends, and financial markets. Accordingly, banks will need to develop more agile organizations across all of the factors above to be able to change their business models and operations faster, and to be able to cope with the increasing competition from inside and outside the banking industry.

Developing the capabilities summarized in Figure 6-3 will require a methodology so that change can be achieved in a sustainable way, without disrupting ongoing operations and adaptation to the marketplace. Given the specifics mentioned above, we recommend the BPM process approach to delivering value, which is based on benchmarking, business process definition, and content management. This approach includes three distinct phases: determining methods and tools, delivering a new model, and transforming the organization. A successful transformation of banks so that they can adapt to, and compete in, the new landscape will, in our view, require:

- A clear and sustained signal from the CEO that sets the tone for cultural and organizational change, and takes responsibility for the current lack of trust in banks and financial institutions. Cultural change inside banks must be embodied by governance throughout the organization and reflected in values and incentives.

- A solid commitment to the principle of value creation for the customer as opposed to narrower measures of profitability or regulatory compliance. The traditional life-cycle approach to banking services must give way to a behavioral and technology-based approach.

- A reinvention of the traditional concept of the branch-centric bank, enabling customers to have the type of interaction with the bank that they prefer.

- A willingness to search for and implement new **strategic alignment** in terms of geographic focus and business mix, in response to shifting demographic and economic trends in the marketplace.

- The need to make certain functions part of everyone's job; these include risk management, customer centricity, and efficiency. These functions should not be circumscribed to one department or unit.

- The need to see regulatory compliance not as a hassle, but rather as an opportunity to create new capabilities that enable the bank or financial institution to compete against its peers.

- The importance of innovating the business model and the application of new technology to address all of the threats and opportunities posed by changing trends, and not merely as an add-on to existing systems and capabilities.

Performance Metrics for a New Banking Business Model

A new business model incorporating the five dimensions of Figure 6-3 will not only require the development of new capabilities, but also a thorough redesign of the main metrics used to measure performance. These will need to consider the interrelationship between the different dimensions and the drivers of change, and include a much wider array of indicators to reflect the expanded set of stakeholders in the banking business beyond investors. Figure 6-4 summarizes our proposal of a much wider set of metrics for performance measurement.

The use of such an integrated set of measures will not only allow banks to get a more comprehensive picture of overall performance, but will also allow for a forward-looking view as to where the bank is heading. Contrary to pure economic or financial measures, which mainly capture ex-post performance, the game-changing nature of the new banking business requires performance indicators that not only visualize how the bank is doing but also how it is preparing for the evolving business landscape.

A FUTURE VISION FOR BANKING—AND HOW TO GET THERE

The global banking landscape has already changed, and will continue to undergo massive changes. National banking ecosystems have also shifted. Banks and financial institutions face a new set of challenges and opportunities. It will be futile for them to adopt a reactive posture. They need to be proactive, to reinvent themselves in a profitable, sustainable, and socially useful business model for banking. One that emerges out of the intersection of demographic, regulatory, economic, and technological drivers of change. Banks cannot afford to play by the same rules they used in the past. The game has shifted, and so must banks.

Figure 6-4. Strategic Dimensions and Performance Metrics

Strategic Dimensions	Performance Metrics
Strategic Alignment	• Geographic/business scope • Market share by area/segment • Economic value added/return on invested capital • Rating/overall risk profile • Reputation index
Incentives	• Capital allocation by business lines • Internal pricing of risk • Capital, solvency, liquidity ratios • Technology expenses to business volume • Penetration in strategic segments • Net customer flow • Customer satisfaction and service quality
Human Resources	• Talent/human capital measures • Employee productivity measures • Cross-employability • Training investment • Payment and incentives policy • Values and diversity
Internal Processes	• Customer lifetime value • Sales productivity • Customer cross-selling and share of wallet • Revenue per customer • Cost-to-income and cost-to-serve • Automation and service productivity • Loan losses and recovery ratios
Customer Interface	• Customer centricity index/customer engagement • Customer satisfaction/Net Promoter Score • Target customer/segment acquisition • Brand recognition • Customer activation/online and mobile penetration • Customer complaints

Source: Accenture, May 2014

Facing Up to Strategic Paradoxes

The combination of strategic issues facing banks across economic, regulatory, competitive, customer, and technological change that we have explored in this book are creating an extraordinarily complex environment for bank leadership. However, it is not just strategic agenda items that are changing. Today's business environment is characterized by both uncertainty and volatility in many of the forces shaping the world. Many of the long-term changes facing banks and other companies, such as the rise of emerging market economies, their populations and their banks, will require fundamental shifts in banks' operating environment. However, some of these changes, both fundamental and uncertain, are happening very fast, such as the shift of customers to digital interaction and competitors to digital business models.

And while bank leaders can map out the strategic challenges and opportunities that they face, this is not a static environment. The response of boards and CEOs can no longer be as straightforward as it was before the crisis, when a growth focus dominated boardrooms. Now, to successfully navigate the landscape after the battle, banks must satisfy multiple objectives. In part, this means that banks must better meet the needs of a wider set of stakeholders, fulfilling the needs of their owners while also those of their regulators, customers, and the societies they touch. In part, it is a matter of finding a sustainable path to growth while negotiating a more complex business environment, with a renewed focus on risk management and business sustainability. And, in part, it is building a business and operating model that is fit for the digital era. This is a new agenda, and it is one that is fraught with paradoxes.

- Banks face a wide range of new regulations that impose a significant set of changes on business strategy, the operating model, and culture. For most banks, the need to raise capital and repair balance sheets comes at the same time that they are being pressured to extend new lending to support fragile economies. Attempts to rationalize global operating and risk-management models to manage regulation across an institution are challenged by the fact that, despite global regulatory principles, banks face diverging local or regional implementation of new rule books.

And as they attempt to return to growth through winning more business from their existing corporate, business, and retail customers, new regulations ranging from ring fencing to revisiting the capital intensity of certain businesses to new conduct of business rules are leading banks to constrain or withdraw from some business areas. Further, most banks must invest large sums in their technology and business processes to comply with regulation, at the same time they need to find investment for technology upgrades and innovation to keep up with new competition and growing customer expectations.

• Trust and legitimacy with customers, regulators, and staff have all been hit through a crisis that was as much reputational as financial. Yet, banks must recover customer and stakeholder trust to earn the right to do more business with their existing customers and extend their services to become true partners in their customers' lives. To find new growth, they may pursue new customer groups, such as the unbanked who may inherently distrust them. They must also fix products, sales processes, and incentives to become fairer and more transparent with customers, not just to regain trust but to avoid future mis-selling or market manipulation scandals, while at the same time increasing sales productivity to grow top line revenues. And further with the reputational hit and scrutiny on pay and increasing demand for high-value technical skills, banks must compete for the top talent from new entrants to leadership at a time that working in the sector has become less attractive to many.

• At the same time as regulators around the world are reconsidering the competitiveness of the banking industry, companies from an increasing number of business sectors and new entrants are looking to gain a foothold in financial services. As a result, a number of the barriers of entry to banking are lowering. In some cases, banks will need to enable new entrants more access to key banking infrastructure, such as payments utilities, but at the same time they must develop new ways to compete for customers and differentiate their services.

As banking digitalizes and customer interactions and data flows increase, banks will need to become more like data processing companies in the way they manage data and provide services to their customers, while fending off competition from new and converging entrants, many of which, such as telecommunications and tech companies, are data processing leaders. Some of the new entrants are already experimenting with radically new economic and business models; just as Google reinvented advertising and Apple challenged the music business, banks must determine whether new revenue models for financial services are viable, while defending and expanding their existing ones.

• Many customer growth and revenue opportunities will lie in emerging markets, however most Western banks have been narrowing the focus of their international businesses and concentrating their capital to support growth in core markets. Within many developing markets, banks face particular challenges to capture new growth opportunities. Their corporate, institutional, and wealthier customers are demanding more sophisticated and complex products and services, while new customer groups, including the low-income strata and emerging middle classes, require more affordable mass market products delivered at lower costs.

Meanwhile, growing emerging market giants are increasingly looking to overseas markets; and while establishing a presence in Western markets is important for extending capital market access and trade, the returns on offer in other emerging markets may be much greater. Regardless of home territory, banks' intentions to access growth opportunities in overseas markets and their attempts to develop common regional or international operating models meet a countervailing trend of increased local regulation and more frequent domestic subsidiarization and branching rules.

The industry as a whole also faces a profitability challenge. In most developed markets, profitability is low and is forecast to remain so in the near future; while in many emerging markets where profitability has been supported by healthy margins, policy and competition are driving margins lower. At the same time that banks need to restore or maintain profitability, they are being required to raise capital levels to support their existing balance sheets, increasing the denominator on the ROE calculation.

Facing revenue and asset-growth constraints, banks will need to look to their cost structure to improve profitability performance. Most banks continue to maintain a heavy cost structure to support universal services to their customers through branch networks. These are valuable assets even as more customer interaction goes digital, and yet they must also be prepared to compete with nimble and light niche competitors that are innovating new business models to compete with the incumbents. And at the same time, banks will need to refresh and upgrade technology and exercise greater control of their risk assets and management but avoid large increases in their fixed costs.

New Principles for the New Landscape

Navigating this complex environment and its inherent paradoxes will create winners and losers. However, due to the heterogeneous nature of domestic markets, global forces, and bank business models, there are no easy, one-size-fits-all solutions to sever the Gordian knot of strategic complexity. However, we think there is a set of principles that are emerging for high-performing banks.

Traditional management disciplines will continue to have their place—the alignment of balance-sheet management to the economic cycle, growing customer relationships over a lifetime, and managing complex liquidity cycles. Many of the changes that have developed over the last decade, such as embracing novel ways to interact with customers through emerging technology channels and the move to rethink retail banking with the logic of retailers, will continue to play their role. However, a new set of principles will be needed to guide leading organizations through the next decades.

- **Stakeholder value creation.** Banks will need to have a broader focus on the outputs and outcomes of their business, between public, regulator, investor, and customer outcomes, to rebuild legitimacy and reflect the social contract implicit in the relationships between states and banks. These outcomes are likely to include economic growth, financial inclusion, and customer engagement as well as sustainable shareholder value creation—and they will be mediated by increased transparency, governance, and values-based management.

- **Rethinking customer focus.** Increasing availability of information has increased consumer power across all consumer businesses; together with a renewed focus on customer protection, this will require banks to truly put customers at the heart of the business. This will mean thinking through business models focused on broad customer needs; in retail this may mean lifestyle, lifetime, and economic needs, and moving away from a focus on financial product sales. In some cases, this will shift revenue models, processes, and behaviors toward a more equitable sharing of value with customers and toward partnership-based advice.

- **Strategic balance-sheet management.** The new regulatory framework will mean that banks need a renewed focus on economic profit and risk balancing across their business and with their partners in the financial ecosystem. It is both a macro and a micro game. At the most strategic level, banks are likely to have to make more dynamic decisions about which markets and business lines to grow or shrink. At the operational level, it will require that the cost of capital, liquidity, and funding is fully incorporated into the pricing and product usage and across businesses. These disciplines will need to be embedded into risk management as well as frontline behaviors, especially in capital markets, business banking, and advice-based sales.

- **An information business.** Banking has always been an information business, but new capabilities and the pervasiveness of technology are changing the paradigm of information technology from a tool to a strategic capability. As discussed in chapter 5, digital technology has the capacity to revolutionize relationships and financial access. Yet from high-frequency trading to retail customer interactions to monetizing vast banking data stores, information technology is now defining business models and increasing competitive advantage too.

- **Newly contestable markets.** Cross-industry convergence and start-up disruption are remaking customer markets, particularly those where large information flows can be disintermediated or value chains reshaped through technology. Financial services are being targeted by technology firms and traditional firms with large customer bases, as well as financial technology start-ups. Banks will increasingly need to be aware of new competition and build in the agility to change or co-opt novel business models, either through innovation, partnership, or acquisition.

- **Strategic agility.** The growing interconnection of global markets and international capital flows require banks to be constantly vigilant and quick to move positions. The combination of emerging forces and pace of change also requires bank to build more speed and flexibility into their business models. Many banks are beset by historical business, process, and technical complexity that add costs and slow change. But increasingly they will need to adapt to new market or competitive forces in a timely, cost-effective, and risk-aware fashion. A new operating platform is required, and it is not all about cost, although cost management will remain essential. Banks will need to move from asset-heaving business models, where they own and build the majority of their capabilities, toward sourcing the components of their business, and even their workforce, from a wider array of suppliers and utilities that they can scale up or down as the need arises—such as the new creators and disseminators of information.

A Vision for the Future

Our vision requires that banks do things differently. Banks are essential actors in the economy, and as yet there is no answer for a better system for the breadth and scale of services that banks provide their customers and the economy. But more than ever before, regulators, innovators, and banks are questioning how things are done.

The scale and pace of change raises the question of the future of banks. Could they be outcompeted? Could they be replaced? It has happened to other industries. These include regulatory monopolies or oligopolies, particularly where companies were vertically and horizontally integrated, and particularly where they were considered too big to fail. Or those whose business and operating models did not keep pace with key changes in technology or customer preference. Think Standard Oil Co. Inc., Swissair S.A./AG, Eastman Kodak Company, Borders Group Inc., HMV Retail Ltd, Blockbuster LLC.

For the banking industry, particularly in the West, many of these conditions are apparent. Is the future role of banks to become utility providers among many essential financial services—at low cost and with little differentiation? Or can they maintain a privileged position of trust and close relationship with their customers?

A way forward is to learn from the transformations that have occurred in other industries. Just-in-time manufacturing approaches focused on improving business performance by reducing waste throughout the production chain. Developed in Japan in the 1970s and widely embraced around the world in manufacturing industries, just-in-time (JIT) allowed companies to revolutionize their cost base, increase flexibility, and increase focus on customer requirements such as quality. Through a combination of techniques—including improving demand forecasting, continual process improvement, and integrating supply chains to reduce inventory—JIT became a key philosophy behind modern manufacturing techniques and has been applied to numerous industries and business processes.

A similar approach can now be applied to the banking industry to increase customer focus, efficiency, and flexibility. As banking becomes increasingly digitalized, as customers use banking services more frequently, and as banks integrate with commercial clients' financial supply chains, interactions and transactions will dramatically increase. The bank will also need to capture these interactions across more channels and through different partners, making the servicing environment more complex. And many of these interactions will offer less immediate revenue opportunity but require richer information from inside and outside the organization. A traditional bank model will struggle to assemble and process these interactions at the speed or low transaction costs required.

As customers demand increasingly complex and personalized services, both for retail and corporate, banks need to combine deep customer analytics with the ability to dynamically assemble the right products and services from within and outside the organization, without creating bespoke services. A just-in-time bank could respond to these challenges by building the customer service offering and information requirements in real time through a new technology-enabled operating platform. By building a series of managed service operations and cloud computing applications, together with modern core banking technology, the bank could extend and integrate supply chains to meet customer needs at the point of demand, without building and owning all the capabilities and infrastructure itself. These services could range from document processing and payments through to analytics, customer management, and even agent distribution, and draw on industry standard services and technology providers in the market today.

Instead of building services to manage "peak load," the bank would instead need to scale up and down the internal and external network of suppliers to assemble services at the point of the customers need—and price these services variably, rather than investing large sums in fixed-cost infrastructure, technology, and people. A critical enabler is automating the bank's business processes as far as possible to reduce manual interventions, facilitate information flows in real time, and automate controls, risk management, and analytics.

Fine-tuning the operating model toward a JIT banking engine would give the banks improved control and understanding of the embedded costs of its operating model, as processes and services are measured and priced across the supply chain. And by moving toward a model in which services are assembled, banks ought to be able to reconfigure products, processes, and services to move with a more dynamic market. And by tuning the engine, bank management and staff can refocus their efforts on managing their critical challenges of customer relationships, risk, and balance sheets, while navigating their strategic journey through the landscape after the battle.

Notes

Chapter 1

1. Gregory R. Samanez-Larkin, "Financial Decision Making and the Aging Brain," *Observer* 26 (5) (May/June 2013), accessed August 17, 2013, http://www.psychologicalscience.org/index.php/publications/observer/2013/may-june-13/financial-decision-making-and-the-aging-brain.html.
2. S. Agarwal, J. C. Driscoll, X. Gabaix, and D. I. Laibson, "The Age of Reason: Financial Decisions Over the Life-Cycle with Implications for Regulation," *Brookings Papers on Economic Activity,* 40 (2009): 51–117.
3. A. Luzardo and O. S. Mitchell, "Financial Literacy and Retirement Planning in the United States," *Journal of Pension Economics and Finance* 10(4) (2011).
4. Capgemini and Merrill Lynch Global Wealth Management, *World Wealth Report 2011* (2011).
5. Zheng Liu and Mark M. Spiegel, "Boomer Retirement: Headwinds for U.S. Equity Markets?" Federal Reserve Bank of San Francisco, Economic Letter 2011-26.
6. Capgemini and RBC Wealth Management, *World Wealth Report 2013* (2013), 7.
7. Asli Demirgüç-Kunt, Leora F. Klapper, and Dorothe Singer, *Financial Inclusion and Legal Discrimination Against Women: Evidence from Developing Countries*, World Bank Policy Research Working Paper No. 6416 (April 1, 2013).
8. Homi Kharas, *The Emerging Middle Class in Developing Countries*, OECD (2010).

9. Pew Research Center, *Millennials: A Portrait of Generation Next* (February 2010).

Chapter 2

1. Some recent examples in this direction are: Switzerland re-examining its own bank capital rules; U.S. pursuing its own subsidiarization rules with some foreign banks, such as Deutsche Bank, changing its U.S. investment banking structure to no longer be a fully licensed bank; U.K. differences with the rest of Europe regarding FTT and caps on bank bonus.

2. Andrew Haldane, Bank of England, "The Contribution of the Financial Sector—Miracle or Mirage?" annex to speech given at the Future of Finance Conference in London, July 14, 2010.

3. Andrew G. Haldane, Bank of England, "On Being the Right Size," speech at Institute of Economic Affairs' 22nd Annual Series, The 2012 Beesley Lectures at the Institute of Directors, Pall Mall, October 25, 2012, http://www.bankofengland.co.uk/publications/Pages/speeches/default.aspx.

4. Mike Mariathasan and Ouarda Merrouche, "Capital Adequacy and Hidden Risk," *Vox: Research-Based Policy Analysis and Commentary from Leading Economists,* June 2013, http://www.voxeu.org/article/capital-adequacy-and -hidden-risk?quicktabs_tabbed_recent_articles_block=0.

5. Haldane, "On Being the Right Size."

6. *High-Level Expert Group on Reforming the Structure of the E.U. Banking Sector,* chaired by Erkki Liikanen, Final Report, Brussels, October 2, 2012.

7. Olena Havrylchyk and Gunther Capelle-Blancard, "The Ability of Banks to Shift Taxes to Their Customers," *LabeX ReFi,* April 2013.

Chapter 3

1. "China's Big Banks: Giant Reality-Check," *The Economist*, August 31, 2013.

2. Arnold W. A. Boot and Anjan V. Thakor, "Financial System Architecture," *The Review of Financial Studies,* 10 (3) (Autumn, 1997): 693–733.

3. Stephen G. Cecchetti and Enisse Kharroubi, "Reassessing the Impact of Finance on Growth," BIS Working Papers No 381, Monetary and Economic Department, July 2012.

4. Andrew Haldane, Bank of England, "The Contribution of the Financial Sector—Miracle or Mirage?" annex to speech given at the Future of Finance Conference in London, July 14, 2010.

5. *McKinsey on Finance*, Number 47, Summer 2013.

6. Allen N. Berger and Loretta J. Mester, "Inside the Black Box: What Explains

Differences in the Efficiencies of Financial Institutions?" *Journal of Banking and Finance,* July 21, 1997, 895–947.

7. Andrew G. Haldane, Bank of England, "On Being the Right Size," speech at Institute of Economic Affairs' 22nd Annual Series, The 2012 Beesley Lectures at the Institute of Directors, Pall Mall, October 25, 2012.

8. Loretta J. Mester and Joseph P. Hughes, "Who Said Large Banks Don't Experience Scale Economies? Evidence from a Risk-Return-Driven Cost Function," *Journal of Financial Intermediation,* 22 (October 2013): 559-585.

9. TNS Global, "Stopping the Itch to Switch—Why Retail Banking Can't Bank on Customer Loyalty," 2013, http://www.tnsglobal.com/other-news/stopping -itch-switch-why-retail-banking-can%E2%80%99t-bank-customer-loyalty -part-2.

10. Payments Council, "Results Published Covering First Three Months of New Current Account Switch Service," January 16, 2014, http://www .paymentscouncil.org.uk/media_centre/press_releases/-/page/2798/.

11. Francisco Gonzalez, "Banks Need to Take on Amazon and Google or Die," *Financial Times,* March 12, 2013.

12. Thomas Philippon and Ariell Reshef, *Wages and Human Capital in the U.S. Financial Industry: 1909-2006,* New York University, 2011.

13. Financial Stability Board, "Strengthening Oversight and Regulation of Shadow Banking," August 29, 2013.

14. *The Economist,* "Shadow Banking in China: Credit Paroled," February 1, 2014, http://www.economist.com/news/finance-and-economics/21595483 -big-default-averted-credit-paroled; Charles Riley, "China's $500 Million Shadow Bank Rescue," CNN.com, January 28, 2014, http://money.cnn .com/2014/01/28/investing/china-icbc-default/.

Chapter 4

1. Accenture and Efma, *REBanking: Insight for Banks from the Retailing Sector* (2013); Capgemini, *2012 Retail Banking Voice of the Customer Survey.*

2. Sandra L. Suárez, "Reciprocal Policy Diffusion: The Regulation of Executive Compensation in the UK and the US," *Journal of Public Affairs* (2012).

3. Capgemini, *2012 Retail Banking Voice of the Customer Survey.*

4. Jonathan Camhi, "Convenience No. 1 Factor in Customer Loyalty for Banks, Study Finds," *Bank Systems & Technology,* accessed August 23, 2013, http://www.banktech.com/channels/convenience-no-1-factor-in-customer -loya/240154006; Bain & Co., *Customer Loyalty in Retail Banking* (2012).

Chapter 5

1. Juan Pedro Moreno, "Banking at a Digital Crossroads," *Financial Times*, January 28, 2014.

2. Accenture, *2013 Innovation Survey.*

3. Aite Group, From the report: "The Global Rise of Smartphonatics: Driving Mobile Payment and Banking Adoption in the United States, EMEA, and Asia-Pacific," published May 2012, http://www.aitegroup.com/report/global -rise-smartphonatics-driving-mobile-payment-and-banking-adoption -united-states-emea-and.

4. GSMA, *State of the Industry: Results from the 2012 Global Mobile Money Adoption Survey* (2012).

5. Ernst & Young, *Global Consumer Banking Survey* (2012).

6. comScore, *Financial Services MobiLens Re-Contact Survey*, April-June 2011.

7. First Data, "First Data Global Study Reveals That Consumers Worldwide Seek the Same Technology Experience," June 19, 2013, accessed July 20, 2013, http://www.firstdata.com/en_us/about-first-data/media/press-releases/ 06_19_13.html.

8. Joel Berg, "Social Media Most Likely to Lead to Your Bank's Next Sale," *American Banker*, August 1, 2013.

9. Asli Demirguc-Kunt and Lora F. Klapper, *Measuring Financial Inclusion,* World Bank Policy Research Working Paper No. 6025 (2012).

10. Mary Wisniewski, "Consumers More Willing to Pay for Mobile Banking: Study," *American Banker,* June 24, 2013.

11. McKinsey, *Micro-, Small and Medium-Sized Enterprises in Emerging Markets: How Banks Can Grasp a $350 Billion Opportunity* (2012).

12. Accenture, *Mobile Banking Case Studies* (2010); Bain & Company, *The Digital Challenge to Retail Banks* (2012).

13. Berg, "Social Media Most Likely to Lead to Your Bank's Next Sale.

14. Accenture, *Mobile Banking Case Studies.*

15. Accenture, *Mobile Banking Case Studies*; Accenture, *Consumer Mobile Payments Survey 2013.*

16. Accenture and Efma, *Insight First! Leveraging Analytics to Engage with Customers* (2010).

17. Accenture, *Consumer Mobile Payments Survey 2013.*

18. Accenture and Efma, *REBanking: Insight for Banks from the REtailing Sector* (2013).

References

Accenture. *2013 Innovation Survey.*

Accenture and Efma. *Insight First! Leveraging Analytics to Engage with Customers* (2010).

Accenture and Efma. *REBanking: Insight for Banks from the Retailing Sector* (2013); Capgemini, *2012 Retail Banking Voice of the Customer Survey.*

Accenture. *Consumer Mobile Payments Survey 2013.*

Accenture. *Mobile Banking Case Studies* (2010); Bain & Company, *The Digital Challenge to Retail Banks* (2012).

Accenture. *Mobile Banking Case Studies*; Accenture, *Consumer Mobile Payments Survey 2013.*

Agarwal, S., J. C. Driscoll, X. Gabaix, and D. I. Laibson, "The Age of Reason: Financial Decisions Over the Life-Cycle with Implications for Regulation." *Brookings Papers on Economic Activity.* 40 (2009): 51–117.

Aite Group. The Global Rise of Smartphonatics: Driving Mobile Payment and Banking Adoption in the United States, EMEA, and Asia-Pacific, published May 2012, http://www.aitegroup.com/report/global-rise-smartphonatics-driving-mobile -payment-and-banking-adoption-united-states-emea-and

Berg, Joel. "Social Media Most Likely to Lead to Your Bank's Next Sale," *American Banker*, August 1, 2013.

Berger, Allen N. and Loretta J. Mester, "Inside the Black Box: What Explains Differences in the Efficiencies of Financial Institutions?," *Journal of Banking and Finance,* July 21, 1997, 895–947

Boot, Arnold W.A., and Anjan V. Thakor, "Financial System Architecture," *The Review of Financial Studies,* 10 (3) (Autumn, 1997): 693–733

References

Camhi, Jonathan. "Convenience No. 1 Factor in Customer Loyalty for Banks, Study Finds," *Bank Systems & Technology,* accessed August 23, 2013, http://www.banktech.com/channels/convenience-no-1-factor-in-customer-loya/240154006; Bain & Co., *Customer Loyalty in Retail Banking* (2012).

Capgemini, *2012 Retail Banking Voice of the Customer Survey.*

Capgemini and Merrill Lynch Global Wealth Management. *World Wealth Report 2011* (2011).

Capgemini and RBC Wealth Management. *World Wealth Report 2013* (2013), 7.

Cecchetti, Stephen G. and Enisse Kharroubi, "Reassessing the Impact of Finance on Growth," BIS Working Papers No 381, Monetary and Economic Department, July 2012.

"China's Big Banks: Giant Reality-Check," *The Economist*, August 31, 2013.

comScore. Financial Services MobiLens Re-Contact Survey, April-June 2011.

Demirgüç-Kunt, Asli, Leora F. Klapper, and Dorothe Singer, *Financial Inclusion and Legal Discrimination Against Women: Evidence from Developing Countries.* World Bank Policy Research Working Paper No. 6416 (April 1, 2013).

Demirguc-Kunt, Asli and Lora F. Klapper, *Measuring Financial Inclusion,* World Bank Policy Research Working Paper No. 6025 (2012).

Ernst & Young. *Global Consumer Banking Survey* (2012).

Financial Stability Board. "Strengthening Oversight and Regulation of Shadow Banking," August 29, 2013

First Data. "First Data Global Study Reveals That Consumers Worldwide Seek the Same Technology Experience," June 19, 2013, accessed July 20, 2013, http://www.firstdata.com/en_us/about-first-data/media/press-releases/06_19_13.html.

Gonzalez, Francisco."Banks Need to Take on Amazon and Google or Die," *Financial Times*, March 12, 2013.

GSMA, *State of the Industry: Results from the 2012 Global Mobile Money Adoption Survey* (2012).

Haldane, Andrew G., Bank of England, "The Contribution of the Financial Sector—Miracle or Mirage?" annex to speech given at the Future of Finance Conference in London, July 14, 2010.

Haldane, Andrew G., Bank of England, "On Being the Right Size," speech at Institute of Economic Affairs' 22nd Annual Series. The 2012 Beesley Lectures at the Institute of Directors, Pall Mall, October 25, 2012, http://www.bankofengland.co.uk/publications/Pages/speeches/default.aspx.Kharas, Homi, *The Emerging Middle Class in Developing Countries*, OECD (2010).

References

Haldane, Andrew G., Bank of England, "On Being the Right Size," speech at Institute of Economic Affairs' 22nd Annual Series, The 2012 Beesley Lectures at the Institute of Directors, Pall Mall, October 25, 2012

Haldane, "On Being the Right Size."

Havrylchyk, Olena and Gunther Capelle-Blancard, "The Ability of Banks to Shift Taxes to Their Customers," *LabeX ReFi,* April 2013.

High-Level Expert Group on Reforming the Structure of the E.U. Banking Sector, chaired by Erkki Liikanen, Final Report, Brussels, October 2, 2012.

Kharas, Homi, "The Emerging Middle Class in Developing Countries," OECD (2010).

Liu, Zheng and Mark M. Spiegel, "Boomer Retirement: Headwinds for U.S. Equity Markets?" Federal Reserve Bank of San Francisco, Economic Letter 2011-26.

Luzardo, A., and O. S. Mitchell, "Financial Literacy and Retirement Planning in the United States." *Journal of Pension Economics and Finance* 10(4) (2011).

Mariathasan, Mike and Ouarda Merrouche, "Capital Adequacy and Hidden Risk," Vox: Research-Based Policy Analysis and Commentary from Leading Economists, June 2013, http://www.voxeu.org/article/capital-adequacy-and -hidden-risk?quicktabs_tabbed_recent_articles_block=0.

McKinsey. *Micro-, Small and Medium-Sized Enterprises in Emerging Markets: How Banks Can Grasp a $350 Billion Opportunity* (2012).

McKinsey on Finance, Number 47, Summer 2013.

Mester, Loretta J. and Joseph P. Hughes, "Who Said Large Banks Don't Experience Scale Economies? Evidence from a Risk-Return-Driven Cost Function," *Journal of Financial Intermediation,* 22 (October 2013): 559-585.

Moreno, Juan Pedro "Banking at a Digital Crossroads," *Financial Times,* January 28, 2014.

Payments Council. "Results Published Covering First Three Months of New Current Account Switch Service," January 16, 2014, http://www.paymentscouncil.org .uk/media_centre/press_releases/-/page/2798/.

Pew Research Center. *Millennials: A Portrait of Generation Next* (February 2010).

Philippon, Thomas and Ariell Reshef, *Wages and Human Capital in the U.S. Financial Industry: 1909-2006,* New York University, 2011.

Samanez-Larkin, Gregory R., "Financial Decision Making and the Aging Brain." *Observer* 26 (5) (May/June 2013), accessed August 17, 2013, http://www .psychologicalscience.org/index.php/publications/observer/2013/may- june-13/financial-decision-making-and-the-aging-brain.html.

References

Suárez, Sandra L. "Reciprocal Policy Diffusion: The Regulation of Executive Compensation in the UK and the US," *Journal of Public Affairs* (2012).

The Economist, "Shadow Banking in China: Credit Paroled," February 1, 2014, http://www.economist.com/news/finance-and-economics/21595483-big-default-averted-credit-paroled; Charles Riley, "China's $500 Million Shadow Bank Rescue," CNN.com, January 28, 2014, http://money.cnn.com/2014/01/28/investing/china-icbc-default/.

TNS Global, "Stopping the Itch to Switch—Why Retail Banking Can't Bank on Customer Loyalty," 2013, http://www.tnsglobal.com/other-news/stopping-itch-switch-why-retail-banking-can%E2%80%99t-bank-customer-loyalty-part-2

Wisniewski, Mary. "Consumers More Willing to Pay for Mobile Banking: Study," *American Banker*, June 24, 2013.

Index

Index

Index

Index

About the Authors

Angel Berges is a professor of finance and international management at Universidad Autónoma de Madrid, as well as professor of finance at AFI-Escuela de Finanzas. He is a founding partner and CEO at AFI. He has published more than one-hundred fifty articles, with over fifty in scientific journals including the *Journal of Finance*, and over twelve books including co-authoring the recent *Innovation, Technology and Finance*. He is a former Fulbright Scholar, and received his PhD at Purdue University. He is past vice president and past president of the European Finance Association. He was a member of the Selection Committee at the IBEX, the Spanish Stock Exchange Index. Since June 2011, he has served as a member of the Stakeholders Group at the European Securities Markets Authority (ESMA).

Mauro F. Guillén is the Zandman Professor of International Management at the Wharton School, and the Director of the Lauder Institute of Management and International Studies. His research deals with the internationalization of companies and banks, with special emphasis on cultural and institutional aspects. He has written over ten books and thirty scholarly articles, including *Global Turning Points* (with Emilio Ontiveros), and *Emerging Markets Rule* (with Esteban García-Canal). He is a former Fulbright and Guggenheim Fellow, and a member in the Institute for Advanced Study at Princeton. He is the winner of the Aspen Institute's Faculty Pioneer Award.

He serves on the Advisory Board of the School of Applied Finance at Analistas Financieros Internacionales, and on the World Economic Forum's Global Agenda Council on Emerging Multinationals.

Juan Pedro Moreno is Accenture's senior managing director—Global Banking, and is responsible for the industry group's overall vision and strategy, investment priorities, offering development and supporting network of alliance partners. Mr. Moreno has built his career serving clients in the financial services industry. He has been responsible for large-scale transformation projects at banking and capital markets firms in Europe, North America, South America, and Africa, with a special focus on trading architectures and central banks. Since joining Accenture in 1989, Mr. Moreno has held leadership positions related to client account excellence, innovation, and diversity. He has been responsible for some of Accenture's largest banking client relationships. In addition, Mr. Moreno serves as an Innovation and Economics Chair at Universidad Autónoma de Madrid, where he holds a degree in economics and business administration. He is an Eisenhower Fellow.

Emilio Ontiveros is Professor of Economic and Business Administration at the Universidad Autónoma de Madrid since 1985, where he has been Vice Chancellor for the past four years. He is Founder and President of Analistas Financieros Internacionales. He has authored and co-authored several books and numerous articles. He has served as contributor and editorial board member for numerous magazines specializing in international economics and finance. Since its creation, he has been director of *The Economist* magazine, published by the Colegio de Economistas de Madrid until December 2011. Recent books: *Global Turning Points: Understanding the Challenges for Business in the 21st. Century* (Cambridge University Press), 2012, *Una nueva época. Los grandes retos del siglo XXI* (Galaxia Gutenberg), 2012,*El Rescate* (Aguilar), 2013, and *El ahorrador inteligente* (Espasa) 2014.